IT'S OKAY TO BE AN IDIOT

DUSTIN PORTILLO

www.DustinMPortillo.com

Cover design by Dustin Portillo

Copy editing by Sage Brawn

ISBN 979-8-89298-358-7 (softcover)

ISBN 979-8-89342-686-1 (e-book)

Forward

If you are looking for inspiration, guidance, and living proof that the pathway to making dreams come true is realistic and attainable, then keep reading. I can say that with authority as I had a ringside seat watching Dusting Portillo transition from the world of entertainment to the corporate headquarters of one of the largest McDonald's franchises in the country. The way he details in this book his unique journey from childhood dreamer to business executive may be one of his greatest performances with which you can insert your own goals and aspirations on a path of achievement.

When Dustin arrived at our corporate office, I already had six years of exposure to his exceptional stage presence as a performer and the flawless professionalism with which he executed over a thousand performances. Although it was a risk (we already knew he was an IDIOT) to bring him into our community relations department with zero experience in the corporate world, we believed he embodied the spirit and attitude we were looking for to eventually replace me as I approached retirement.

During one of our first conversations, I congratulated him on his arrival to the new big stage. I assured him he will be required to perform day and night for audiences internally and outside our business. There will be countless hours preparing for performances as you represent nearly 4,000 employees of a cherished community legacy business to the millions of people we serve. The only difference is that you have traded your makeup and costume for a suit and tie.

What followed that conversation was like watching the overnight growth spurt of a 14-year-old. Dustin owned it. He read everything, came in early, stayed late, and volunteered when and where it was needed. Laughter was always the lubricant to open doors and minds and close deals. The sincerity in his desire to help executive leadership, management, employees, guests, and beneficiaries was real. Although I've tried, I cannot thank him enough for all he had done for me as I approached retirement. He took ownership of his new role with authority and intentionality. His personal equity grew as I introduced him to community leaders at corporate events and fundraisers. In short order, the questions transitioned from "who is he" to "where is Dustin?" People just loved to be in his presence as will you as you are fortunate to be in his presence as he helps you grow with the chapters in this book.

Since we parted ways as the community relations team generating happiness both internally and externally at our former employer, we have kept in contact as professionals and friends still doing what we can to help others. This is our common bond. And, as you turn these pages, you will join the community who comes to understand that self-development does not emerge from what you can gain or accomplish from your personal achievement, but by who you can help along the way.

Bob, Ronald McDonald, and me at a Tampa Bay Rays baseball game

To my amazing parents, *Dean and Lisa.* Your love and support have shaped who I am today. Thank you for believing in my childhood dream. I love you both!

Frosty Little, whose belief in me as a rookie clown inspired me to overcome obstacles. His impact on my life will never be forgotten.

Tim Holst, who believed in me and gave me the opportunity to turn my childhood dream into a reality when I was 18 years old.

Bob Conigliaro, your guidance in both the corporate world and life is invaluable. I'm grateful for your support.

To my incredible husband, *Brandon*, your love and presence are a blessing. Thank you for always being there for me and us, Together Forever!

I dedicate this book to all of you. Your love and support have guided me through every major milestone of my life.

MY BROTHER BRANDEN AND ME TRICK-OR-TREATING ON HALLOWEEN, 1993.

id·i·ot

/ˈIDĒƏT/

noun

1. Someone who embraces their uniqueness.
   "I am empowered to embrace being an IDIOT more than ever."

   a. **ARCHAIC**
      a person who confidently owns who they are and the gifts
      they are given.
         "After reading Dustin's book, I fully celebrate my status
         as an unapologetic IDIOT."

The History of the word idiot

The word idiot has a fascinating history, originating from the ancient Greek term "idiotes," which refers to a private citizen not involved in public affairs. Over time, the word's meaning has evolved and taken on new dimensions.

In ancient Greece, an "idiot" was someone who did not participate in public life or contribute to the betterment of society. They were perceived as self-centered and detached from community concerns. However, as language evolved, the word took a different path.

During the Middle Ages, the term "idiot" was often used to describe individuals perceived to lack intelligence or common sense. It was used to describe individuals who were deemed foolish or ignorant. But let's not be deceived by this negative connotation! The word soon embraced a more playful and lighthearted interpretation.

In the 19th century, the term "idiot" underwent another transformation. It became a popular slang word among young people to describe someone acting silly or doing something absurdly funny. It was as if the word had discovered a new lease on life, embracing its own eccentricity and celebrating the joy of being different.

In the present day, the term "idiot" has effortlessly found its way into our daily conversations, often used with a touch of whimsy and amusement.

Contents

Introduction

Buckle up because I'm about to drop a bombshell: I am an absolute IDIOT! I know, it's a big shocker to those familiar with me and probably has everyone else scratching their heads in confusion.

I can already see the quizzical expressions forming on your face! You might be wondering, "Is this person serious?" or questioning whether you should continue reading if indeed I am a total imbecile or a complete dimwit. But hold onto your seat because the answer is a resounding YES!

My idiotic journey began in 1990 when my parents introduced my brother and me to Ringling Bros. and Barnum & Bailey Circus in our hometown of Kansas City . Although I don't personally recollect my first time going to the circus, it has been recounted numerous times that, at the age of 4, I looked up at my parents and confidently declared, "I want to be a clown."

When children are asked about their future careers, they often think of the more conventional professions such as doctors, lawyers, veterinarians, or police officers. Rarely do you come across a child who declares of becoming a circus clown, but surprisingly, such dreams can also come true.

Before I continue, I need to discuss the elephant in the room and debunk the BIGGEST misconception about clowns! Simply putting on exaggerated makeup, funny clothes, oversized shoes, or a red nose makes someone a clown! That would be called stereotyping, which is never a good idea. Certainly, someone can "portray" themselves as a clown just as someone can "portray" themselves as a doctor. It is essential to understand that simply dressing the part does not grant them the necessary qualifications and expertise to embody either profession. To reach the pinnacle in any career, one must possess the virtues of patience, persistence, and practice. These qualities are the hallmarks of individuals who have achieved greatness in their respective fields.

Let's continue…

With unwavering belief and the power of six simple words, "**We become what we think about**," I witnessed the incredible manifestation of making my dream a reality. While many may have chosen a more conventional path after graduating from high school, such as joining the workforce or pursuing higher education, I made the bold decision to break free from societal norms and forge my own destiny. Instead of being confined to four walls and a desk, my office became the three rings of the circus. And while some may joke about working with a bunch of animals, I can say that I truly did.

To this day, I often encounter individuals who remark, "You're so lucky to have fulfilled your childhood dream." However, the word luck has never been a concept I subscribe to. Instead, I firmly believe in the power of preparedness when an opportunity exists. It is the readiness to step into one's own being, embracing one's wholeness and potential. When genuinely prepared, opportunities align with our path, waiting for us to seize them with open arms.

As you delve into the chapters, you'll encounter compelling examples that prompt deep reflection on your life and work. Embrace the opportunity to explore the boundless possibilities within each page. It's a chance to embrace your unique qualities and strengths, forging your path regardless of others' opinions. Embrace the unconventional, challenge the status quo, and let the profound wisdom within these pages ignite a fire within you. As you read my story, I genuinely hope you will embrace the term IDIOT and let it inspire you to achieve greatness by embracing your authentic self.

IMPORTANT: Please note that the word "IDIOT" in the title of this book is not what it seems. Contrary to how the word has been used over time, this book does not promote idiotic ideas or encourage stupidity. We all have moments of both, regardless of whether we read a book. Trust me, I've seen TikTok! The word "IDIOT" has two meanings. Firstly, it refers to a clown or "idiot." Secondly, it represents five fundamental concepts that have profoundly impacted my life and have the potential to revolutionize yours, but only if you are open to receiving.

The book is divided into two parts. The first, Chapters 1-9, explores the interconnected worlds of entertainment and business and reveals that your life is a continuous performance filled with opportunities for growth and success. The second, encompassing Chapters 11-15, delves into the acronym behind the word "IDIOT." Each chapter is dedicated to one of the five fundamental concepts: **IMAGINE** *your potential,* **DREAM** *big,* **IGNITE** *your inner fire, own your* **ORIGINALITY**, and *give* **THANKS**. These concepts serve as guiding principles to unleash your true potential and lead a more fulfilling life.

No matter where you are in your journey - whether you're feeling lost in a role that no longer brings you fulfillment, you've become complacent, or you're searching for the next significant career move- this book guides and inspires you. It offers valuable insights and practical advice to help you rediscover your purpose and find the motivation to thrive. This book has something to offer you on your path to personal and professional growth.

I'm excited for you to dive into this book, so I won't keep you waiting any longer with a lengthy introduction.

Let's go, the show is about to begin!

Chapter 1

Stepping Into the Spotlight: The Circus Calls

Growing up, I had what would be considered a "typical" childhood. I enjoyed playing video games, riding my bike, and playing with my Hot Wheels cars. At first glance, I seemed just like any other kid in our neighborhood. However, deep inside me, a burning desire could not be contained. After school, I found immense fulfillment in putting on my plaid green pajamas and immersing myself in the role of a circus clown; from the outside, this is called playing make-believe. I'd often imagine myself playing out various parts of the circus or getting hit in the face by a pie like the heroes I came to idolize. It was something that genuinely sparked joy within me.

One particular memory I vividly recall is the arrival of the Ringling Bros. and Barnum & Bailey Circus train at the Kansas City stockyards next to Kemper Arena, where the show had played for decades. Every year, in early September, my parents would take us kids on a drive across town to witness the magnificent sight of the train. This unique tradition always happened on a Tuesday evening, after rush hour, as the sun faded behind the skyscrapers of downtown Kansas City. The train yard lights created a captivating illumination, beautifully highlighting the painted red banner with white metallic lettering, which read, "Ringling Bros. and Barnum & Bailey, The Greatest Show On Earth." The banner extended along the length of each train car, adding to its visual appeal. Tuesday late afternoon/early evening is when the train would pull into town and begin the load-in process of the show. I still remember the incredible feeling I experienced as a child when I saw that train. Remember Ralph from *A Christmas Story* when he saw the Red Ryder Carbine Action BB gun in the storefront window? Yes, that was me, minus the shooting your eye out part!

Feld Entertainment, the company that owns Ringling Bros. and Barnum & Bailey Circus, operated two shows, the Red and Blue Unit. Each unit traveled by train, which spanned an impressive mile plus in length and traveled across the country simultaneously throughout the year, showcasing completely different shows. These trains were so extensive that while parked in each city, they were divided into multiple sections to fit on the train tracks. The sight of the train was awe-inspiring, especially as it sat stationary opposite the parking lot of Kemper Arena. Seeing the circus people bustling around the train yard brought a sense of envy as I'd Imagine what it must have been like to live and travel with the circus, experiencing a life filled with wonder and excitement.

RINGLING CLOWN MARK MYERS AND ME AT KEMPER ARENA IN 1999.

After what seemed like an eternity, circus day would finally come. My excitement would be brimming to the point where my father would struggle to park the car quickly enough. I would hastily swing open the car door and eagerly ascend the seemingly never-ending flight of stairs leading to the entrance of the arena. I can still hear my parents yelling at me to, "Slow down and wait for us!" The souvenir stands immediately caught my attention with their enticing items like light-up swords, clown foam hats, and the official souvenir program. The concessionaires, stationed outside in front of the arena's massive glass window entrance would captivate me with their carnival-like script over their loudspeakers announcing, "Ladies and gentlemen, boys and girls, children of all ages, welcome to The Greatest Show On Earth!" I'd grab a program from the stack, eagerly flipping through the pages, and search for the clown section. Like any other kid, I wanted to collect all the souvenirs. Unfortunately, I could only pick one item, which usually ended up being the program.

Over the years, I have watched the performances of clowns, but I never found them uproariously funny. While their gags would occasionally make me chuckle, I was more captivated by the intricacies of their craft. The way they moved, the way they used lighting, live music, and special effects reminded me of listening to a masterpiece by Mozart. The art of clowning fascinated me then, and it still does. It takes a truly talented individual to execute acts like taking a pratfall or throwing a pie with such precision and flawless execution, as the Ringling clowns did.

Each year, after Ringling would load the show and move on, my passion for becoming a clown grew and I'd find myself indulging in playful antics to bring the dream to life. During visits to my grandparents house, I would sneak into their bathroom and gleefully smear my grandfather's Gillette shaving cream on my face, imagining it as clown makeup. I even took my shaving cream escapades to the backyard of my home, creating a mess that never failed to bring my parents to a grinding halt as the backyard would transform into a whimsical and chaotic scene, with soap suds smearing the fence and covering the ground like a blanket of freshly fallen snow. Fueled by my excitement, I would eagerly ask my parents to buy cans of shaving cream, always ready for new mischievous adventures. One birthday, my parents surprised me and ordered professional foam pie shells from a renowned clown prop maker, adding a touch of authenticity to my clowning endeavors. It was an unexpected gift that not only showcased their belief in my dream but also their unwavering support.

After some persuasion, my father reluctantly agreed to join me in the backyard. Equipped with foam pie shells, I would gleefully hurl pie after pie at him, fulfilling my childhood fantasy of being a real clown. The slapstick suds didn't just stay within the boundaries of our home; they spilled over to my grandparents' house as well. During one sud-filled escapade, armed with cans of shaving cream, I ventured into their backyard and drenched myself in buckets of shaving cream. I can still see my great-grandmother looking out the back door, exclaiming to my grandmother, "Loretta, would you just look at the mess he's making back there!"

The unwavering support of both my parents and grandparents laid the foundation for my journey toward becoming the professional clown I had always dreamed of being. On my 15th birthday, I was thrilled to receive my first set of professional clown makeup, juggling balls, and a VHS tape that would teach me the art of juggling. I immediately began honing my newfound skills and within an hour, I had already mastered a few simple tricks.

Each day following that birthday, the moment I stepped through the front door after school, I would excitedly put on my clown makeup. With each stroke of the makeup brush, I could feel the anticipation building. Strolling around the house, honing my skills, and fully embracing the joy of being a clown became a daily ritual.

Back then, I was unaware of the impact my actions would have on my journey, but the practice of visualization shaped my path in ways I couldn't fully grasp. Each day, as I conjured vivid images in my mind of myself as a Ringling Bros. clown, I unknowingly tapped into the power of visualization and the accompanying emotions it brought forth. It became an integral part of my life, a potent combination of visualization and profound emotions that guided me through my formative years. These imaginative exercises nurtured my skills and dreams, creating a deep connection to the enchanting world of clowning. Looking back, I now realize that these seemingly simple acts of visualization played a pivotal role in shaping my journey, instilling in me unwavering confidence and relentless determination to pursue my deepest passion.

I am grateful for the immense power of visualization and its profound impact on my life. It taught me always to **IMAGINE** *your potential* and embrace the exhilarating emotions that accompany the pursuit of one's true calling. Thus, my childhood was enriched with the enchanting magic of visualization, paving the way for a future where I could bestow joy and laughter upon others. Now, more than ever, I firmly believe that consistently engaging in these visualizations transformed my childhood dream into a tangible reality. The first step towards manifesting our desires in life lies in the power of imagination, and then we must wholeheartedly believe in the possibility of its realization. This is the true essence and magic of visualization.

I sincerely thank my parents for their invaluable support and belief in me. They went above and beyond, working extra shifts to provide me with clown wigs, noses, and shoes, which were crucial to my success. Not everyone is fortunate enough to have parents like them, and I will forever be grateful.

As I honed my skills in visualization and tapped into the accompanying emotions, I discovered another talent: eating. However, as my teenage years unfolded, my dreams grew more significant, but so did my waistline. By the time I reached 16, I had found myself at my heaviest weight of 298 pounds. Combined with the realization I was gay, which I had known since the sixth grade, created a toxic mix that haunted my mind. Suicidal thoughts and depression began to engulf me daily as not having someone to turn to, talk to, or confide in posed immense challenges, especially as a teenager.

As I pushed through those tumultuous years, I began to understand the profound truth behind the expression, 'tears of a clown.' This expression perfectly captures the experience of wearing a bright smile while battling inner demons. It reflects the essence of clowns, who effortlessly radiate joy and captivate others, even while dealing with intense emotions beneath the surface. Many comedians openly acknowledge their personal struggles as the foundation for their need to create laughter.

Over time, I gradually I discovered that using humor to bring laughter to others was the most effective form of therapy I could have ever received. In those moments of making others laugh, I found solace and a temporary escape from my struggles. Laughter possesses unparalleled healing powers, capable of mending even the most fragmented fragments of our weary souls. I proudly stand as a living testament to laughter's miraculous and rejuvenating capabilities.

In the summer of 2002, I was fortunate enough to receive a scholarship for the esteemed Mooseburger Clown Arts Camp in Minnesota. This renowned clown school offered intensive courses that would propel me closer to achieving my dream. The camp was magical, from slapstick to movement, juggling to prop-making, and everything in between. While there, I enjoyed meeting Frosty Little, the last living "Master Clown." Frosty had spent 27 years performing with Ringling Bros. and was part of the inaugural graduating class of Clown College in 1968.

Known for his strict and demanding approach to circus clowning, which some deemed "Clown Boot Camp," he was a force to be reckoned with. Despite our insecurities, Frosty expected nothing but excellence from all of us. I vividly recall one day during the week-long program when we worked on a classic boxing gag for the upcoming end-of-week show. Unfortunately, a few other clowns repeatedly made the same mistake. Frosty's patience wore thin and he abruptly halted the gag and said sternly, "If you can't get this damn routine down, quit." I wish I could have seen the expression on my face at that moment. Those words echoed in my head for the remainder of the week. Then and there, I made a firm decision—I would never quit. I consciously decided to relentlessly pursue what I wanted, even if it took longer than expected.

To some, Frosty may have seemed like a "has been" performer whose time in the ring had long passed. But for me, I viewed him as an individual with a keen eye for spotting the hidden potential in people, even when they were unaware of it. Although his tactics may have significantly differed from those of leaders you may have encountered, or even your own, he aimed to discover perfection within what was already good.

FROSTY LITTLE AND ME AT CLOWN CAMP IN 2004.

A few weeks later, after the camp ended and the grease paint was removed, I sent Frosty a letter expressing my gratitude. To my surprise, I received an envelope a few weeks later addressed to me, which I eagerly opened. Inside, I found a two-page letter accompanied by his lengthy resume. As I started reading the first few sentences, I was shocked when I came across the following statement: "First of all, you should lose some weight and get in shape because there is a lot of running in the circus, and everyone else is in good shape." Before this impactful sentence was written, I was already aware that I needed to lose weight; however, it was Frosty's blunt remark that made me realize the situation's urgency.

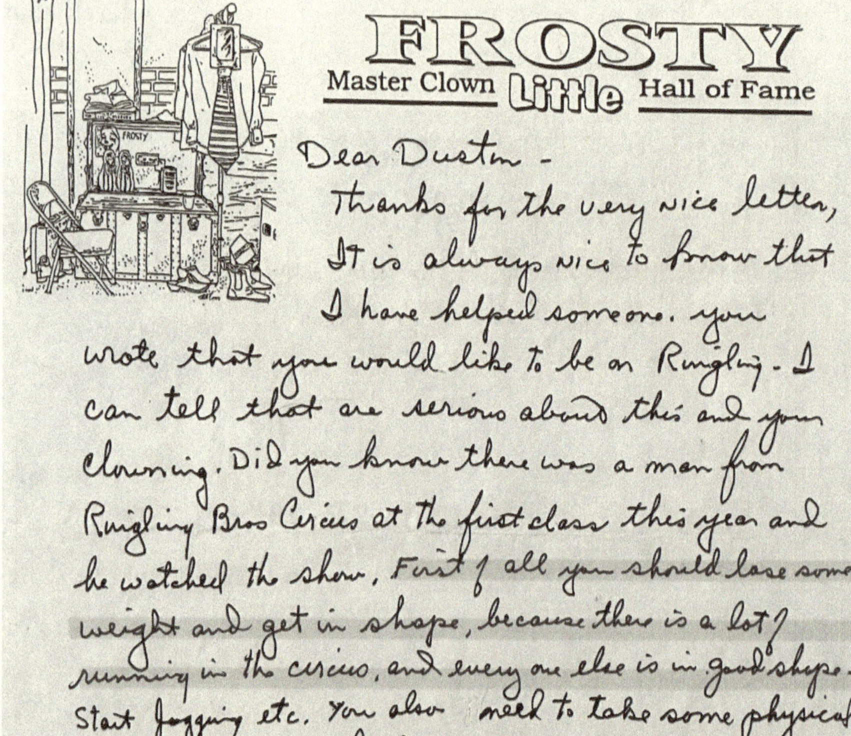

THE LETTER I RECEIVED FROM FROSTY LITTLE, MASTER CLOWN WITH RINGLING BROS. CIRCUS FOR OVER 27 YEARS, CATALYZED MY INCREDIBLE TRANSFORMATION, RESULTING IN A REMARKABLE WEIGHT LOSS OF 127 POUNDS WITHIN NINE MONTHS.

Motivated by his words, I embarked on a nine-month journey during which I managed to lose a staggering 127 pounds and achieve the best physical condition of my life. I experienced a significant transformation in my physical fitness. I went from wearing XXL shirts to mediums and reduced my waist size from 42 inches to 32 inches. To achieve this, I committed to doing 1,000 crunches daily, splitting them into 500 in the morning and 500 at night. I also gradually transitioned from walking to running and included light weights in my exercise routine. I significantly changed my eating habits by eliminating fried food, carbonated beverages, and sweets. But it didn't stop there. I also completely transformed my mindset and overhauled my entire lifestyle.

The letter he sent me many years ago proudly hangs in my house in Tampa, FL. It serves as a reminder of my journey and the progress I have made.

In early 2005, I received a call from one of the instructors at the clown school I had attended the previous year. He offered me a five-month contract for a circus show at the Great Escape, a Six Flags theme park in Queensbury, NY. Knowing my aspirations of becoming a Ringling clown, the instructor wanted to help me gain experience in the world of circus clowning. Up until that point, I had only been involved in local shows, parades, and festivals. Instead of declining the offer out of fear, I saw it as an opportunity to showcase my skills and step outside of my comfort zone. Without any hesitation, I eagerly accepted the opportunity. Interestingly, I discovered in November 2004 that I had enough credits to graduate early, so this incredible opportunity aligned perfectly with my circumstances.

Opting for a Greyhound bus due to the cost of flying, I embarked on a multi-day journey from Kansas City to Bridgeport, CT, where I was scheduled to meet the instructor who had graciously offered me the summer gig.

Over the next five months, I performed under a canvas tent, without air conditioning. I earned a weekly salary of $125, a considerably less paycheck than initially agreed upon. My living accommodations were in the back of a converted Ryder truck, which also served as a dog kennel. My bed was positioned above a six-foot Boa Constrictor, which was used as a photo opportunity after each show for the dog act performer to make a few extra dollars. Every morning, my slumber was abruptly interrupted at 5:30 am by the enthusiastic barking of the performing dogs eagerly anticipating their breakfast. The Ryder truck was not equipped with a bathroom or running water, so each night, once the park had closed, all the guests had exited, and the cleaning crew had made their rounds, I embarked on a ten minute trek to the water park for restroom facilities and a shower.

That summer, I also learned about professionalism and team dynamics. The circus cast consisted of five performers for a 30-minute show, which we performed several times a day, seven days a week. Unfortunately, like in any workplace, drama and tensions can arise. Over those five months, the tension between the other acts reached its boiling point, spilling from backstage to center stage.

One incident that stands out in my memory is when a liquor bottle left in a dressing room was maliciously tied up in the fabric of the aerial performer's chiffon. As she began her act, the plastic bottle fell out in front of the audience, much to my horror. The act responsible for the prank laughed, seemingly proud of their actions. This incident only intensified the rift between the cast members, and I found myself distancing myself from the drama, choosing to live in my bubble for the rest of our contracted dates.

The atmosphere among the cast became somber and tense, which made for a lonely few months until the end of our contract. However, this experience taught me the importance of respecting others and avoiding actions that could harm the team dynamic. Moments like this made me want to quit, but I found strength in the support of my parents through daily calls and care packages. I also kept reminding myself of what Frosty Little would say if he heard me say, "I want to quit."

Prior to the summer gig, I had established a connection with Tim Holst, Vice President of Talent and Production for Feld Entertainment.

Tim was the big shot who hired and fired circus artists. Every year, he traveled over one million miles across the globe, diligently searching for exceptional acts to showcase for Ringling Bros. Circus. His impressive journey from clown to Vice President spanned 37 years. I made it a point to email Tim every month, consistently expressing my unwavering enthusiasm to become a clown with The Greatest Show On Earth.

The last month of my contract at Six Flags, I caught a ride with some of my fellow performers to the local Queensbury library. I intended to access my email, as it had been nearly five months since my last login. As I opened my Yahoo account, I came across an unexpected email from Tim, which he had sent the day before. The subject line caught my attention with the word "Opportunity," and the content of the email was simple: "Call me at your earliest convenience." I dialed Tim's number without much thought, assuming the opportunity had already passed. But to my utter astonishment, Tim offered me a contract to become one of the 14 clowns with Ringling Bros. and Barnum & Bailey Circus.

I received an express package at Six Flags from Feld Entertainment a week later. Excitement coursed through me as I opened it to find a welcome letter and a lengthy contract for the Blue Unit of The Greatest Show On Earth. Deep down, I had always yearned to join the Red Unit, but I couldn't help but be thrilled by this incredible opportunity. I enthusiastically signed the contract and mailed it to Tim Host's secretary. Coincidentally, a friend, Neal Skoy, whom I had met at clown camp a year prior, also received a contract. His childhood dream had always been to become a Ringling clown, just like me, but he was offered a spot in the Red Unit. We shared in each other's joy and couldn't help but feel envy towards the unit we hadn't been chosen for.

It is often said that becoming a Ringling Bros. clown is more challenging than joining the NFL. Ringling only had a limited number of clowns, while the NFL boasts 53 players per team and a combined total of 1,696 across the 32 teams. Knowing your aspirations and setting small, attainable goals is vital in achieving your dreams. Not only does it provide a sense of fulfillment and purpose, but it also nourishes your soul. I knew I had to trust myself and the universe to deliver what I passionately wanted, and nothing would stop me from fulfilling my dream.

After completing my contract with Six Flags in early October, my parents drove halfway across the country to bring me back home to Kansas City. Finally reunited, I settled back into the familiar surroundings of my hometown. That's when an unexpected call came in, informing me of a switch from the Blue to the coveted Red Unit. It was a dream come true. Coincidentally, Neal, too, had been reassigned from the Red to the Blue Unit. Fate had aligned perfectly, granting us our respective desires.

Filled with excitement, I eagerly signed the Red Unit contract two days before my 19th birthday. It was the greatest birthday gift I could have ever asked for. In one month, I would be reporting to Rosemont, IL, a suburb of Chicago, marking the beginning of living out my childhood dream as a professional clown with The Greatest Show On Earth.

SIGNING MY CONTRACT FOR RINGLING BROS. CIRCUS ON OCT. 7, 2005.

Chapter 2

Behind the Makeup:
My Life as a Circus Clown

Having endured the demanding conditions at Six Flags for five months, the living arrangements on Ringling's train felt significantly more comfortable. Whenever I heard others grumble about the living quarters, which were great, I couldn't help but reflect on the difficult living conditions I had endured during those five months. My experience at Six Flags during that time taught me essential lessons in resilience and independence which expedited my growth into adulthood. I was thankful for my prior experience, as it gave me a softer landing to life at Ringling.

The train had different-sized rooms depending on your act or seniority. The smallest of these rooms called "coffins," were incredibly tight spaces where the sink, microwave, and mini refrigerator are within arm's reach from the bed. Each train car had restrooms, showers, and a washer and dryer. I fully embraced my new digs and found solace in not sharing my space with dogs or a snake. New performers like clowns, dancers, and acts with a large group were assigned to these rooms. I experienced a few rooms sizes in seven years until I eventually settled into a quarter car.

The train comprised a total of 61 cars. Among them were 36 coaches, which served as residential cars for the performers and crew.

Additionally, there were two container cars dedicated to storing souvenirs, 19 flat cars for housing 500 tons of equipment and wagons, and four animal cars equipped with water, heating and air conditioning systems to ensure the comfort of the animals in different weather conditions as they traveled from city to city. The train measured 5,049 feet in length, with each car spanning 90 feet. Depending on the train car layout, the number of rooms in each car varied, typically ranging from 4 to 14.

BRANDON AND I ARRIVING IN MY HOMETOWN OF KANSAS CITY, MO, ABROAD ON THE RINGLING BROS. AND BARNUM & BAILEY CIRCUS TRAIN IN 2006.

MY QUARTER CAR ON THE CIRCUS TRAIN WHEN I WAS BOSS CLOWN IN 2012.

While touring, performers encounter numerous obstacles, but one significant challenge involves adjusting to the distinct lifestyle and managing the interpersonal dynamics of living and performing alongside the same group of individuals. The lifestyle involves constant travel for 11 months and performing in 40 cities across North America.

Living and performing alongside the same group of individuals had its rewards and challenges. The circus became our home away from home, and the performers became a close-knit family.

Performers spent countless hours training and rehearsing together, fostering a strong bond and trust within the cast. We relied on each other's skills, timing, and coordination to execute acts flawlessly and safely. This level of teamwork and collaboration proved essential for the success of our performances.

PHOTO CAPTURED MY ENTHUSIASM AFTER MY FIRST WEEK OF SHOWS IN CHICAGO, IL IN 2005.

For many performers, the true challenge often lies in finding their place amidst the chaos and excitement of a show. Many performers who come from smaller productions must adapt to sharing the spotlight with their fellow performers. It is challenging to discover what sets you apart from the rest of the cast in a multimillion-dollar production.

The circus lifestyle also requires performers to maintain high physical and mental fitness. They must follow strict training regimens and care for their bodies to perform at their best. Managing the physical demands of their performances while navigating the trials of touring and life on the road can take a toll on their bodies and emotions. Therefore, self-care becomes paramount to sustain the demanding circus lifestyle.

This constant movement and close-knit community can be both thrilling and demanding. Performers must quickly adapt to new environments, cultural differences, and the logistical challenges of touring. They must be flexible and resourceful, as they often encounter unexpected situations requiring quick thinking and problem-solving skills. Simple everyday tasks we take for granted, like visiting a grocery store, post office, or restaurant, can become challenging for circus performers on the road. They often have to rely on walking to find essential amenities in unfamiliar locations or taking the circus bus on late-night trips to the grocery store every Friday night, just before the three-show Saturday schedule. Living and working as part of a traveling circus can be a unique and fulfilling experience, allowing performers to showcase their talents to a wide range of audiences while immersing themselves in vibrant and diverse communities nationwide.

Here is an outline of what a typical week looked like on tour.

- Monday: Typically a travel day unless our schedule required us to stay in a city for two weeks or more. For week-long stays, like in Tampa, FL, Monday was a travel day to the next city. For longer runs, such as in New York City for a month, Monday was a day off.

- Tuesday: A half-day of travel and a load-in at the arena where we would perform. Load-in was moving animals and equipment from the train to the arena to begin setting up. Loading-in required a workforce of local union workers and performers comprising around 175 people. Some performers, like clowns, dancers, and the ringmaster, would also have public relations appearances on load-in days. We had to transport our wigs, makeup, shoes, and costume pieces on the train. After completing a run in a city, many performers, including myself, had the option to take on additional work known as "cherry pie." This work was not mandatory, but those who chose to participate would be paid $40 for load-in and $40 for load-out. The tasks could vary, ranging from walking the animals, unloading wagons, pulling the ring rubber (a half-inch rubber used to coat the concrete performance area), or assisting with lighting and sound. Overall, the complete transformation of an arena during load-in typically took around 14 hours. It was a busy and exciting process requiring safety, collaboration and coordination, as forgetting a crucial step could prove fatal.

- Wednesday: Opening Night! Run-through and rehearsal of the show. We would go over specific spots in the show that needed adjustments based on the arena's layout. Rehearsing was essential to ensure the smooth flow of the performance. Depending on the city and publicist arrangements, there might be television, newspaper, or radio interviews to promote the show in the morning or later in the afternoon.

- Thursday: This day often started bright and early, as early as 4 or 5 am. We would have early morning television appearances to promote the show further. Sometimes, we had to be up as early as 1 am, especially if the train was parked far from the arena (sometimes up to an hour away) and if multiple stations were doing live hits and teases. Additionally, there might be a special "educational show" in the morning, where local schools would have a buy-out for that day's performance. These shows were always the loudest, with thousands of enthusiastic elementary school kids. In the evening, we would have a regular show.

- Friday: There might be a morning show depending on the city and various public relations appearances scheduled throughout the day. These appearances could include school shows held at school sites, hospital visits, radio station promotions, or occasional parades. And, of course, in the evening, there would be another show.

- Saturday: Brace yourself for a three-show day! Usually, no public relations events were scheduled on this day, allowing the cast and crew to focus solely on delivering incredible performances. It was an exhausting day, but always worth it for the enthusiastic response from the audience.

- Sunday: Another busy day with two shows scheduled. After the last performance, the loading-out process would begin, which typically took about five to six hours. The time required for this process would depend on the venue and any unforeseen circumstances that may arise.

It's important to mention that larger cities like New York City had an even more demanding schedule, filled with local and national public relations events. During the run of the show, there would be 13 to 15 performances per week, often with Friday, Saturday, and Sunday, each consisting of three shows. Including the one-hour pre-show, each performance lasted around three hours with a fifteen-minute intermission. It was a busy and intense schedule, but the energy and excitement of the audience made it all worthwhile.

Warming up the audience before the show begins in 2007.

New York City was always considered the worldwide premiere of the new show despite having already been traveling for three months and having close to 100 shows under your belt. I had the honor of being a part of many national public relations events in New York City, including being featured in articles for *The New York Times, Wall Street Journal,* and other publications.

In addition to our performances, we also took on the responsibility of being ambassadors for the show in each city we visited. As fluent English-speaking performers, we clowns had the opportunity to showcase the show to a range of local and national media outlets. We needed excellent public speaking skills to succinctly communicate our message to thousands of viewers each week effectively.

We underwent rigorous media training yearly to ensure we maintained the highest standards when facing the media. Feld Entertainment would fly in a seasoned news anchor to lead a half-day training session. During these sessions, we would learn the do's and don'ts of media interviews, equipping us with the skills and confidence to handle any media interaction professionally and gracefully.

During the workshop, we learned a valuable skill called "driving the bus" in interviews.

This technique involved taking control of the conversation as performers and guiding it towards our desired outcomes when responding to interview questions. By employing this tactic, we often utilized the entire allocated interview time, leaving little room for additional questions. Furthermore, we were advised to research the interviewer's style thoroughly beforehand, whether they were hard-hitting journalists aiming for newsworthy stories or individuals who preferred a more fun and interactive experience with easy questions.

CLOWNS (L-R) BRANDON FOSTER, NICK RAINONE, AND ME SITTING AT A NEWS DESK AT AN ORLANDO NEWS STATION DURING AN EARLY MORNING PUBLIC RELATIONS APPEARANCE IN 2011.

To prepare for this, each performer underwent a series of mock interviews on the new show, focusing on specific talking points. Running through these mock interviews was critical for performers because it helped them effectively communicate their messages, handle difficult questions, and maintain a positive public image.

Upon learning which public relations appearances we'd be participating in, we would visit the news station's website or listen to the radio shows on YouTube to gain insight into how they conducted interviews. This preparation allowed us to adapt accordingly, as once the workshop concluded, the pressure fell on us to handle any publicity with ease and reassurance while on tour. Media training is an essential component for individuals pursuing a career in the public eye. It guides them to focus on their key points, avoid misunderstandings or misinterpretations, and manage potential crises or negative publicity. It also aids in building confidence and understanding of how the media operates, which can lead to more successful interviews and a better overall relationship with the media.

Doing interviews was both a blessing and a challenge for me. As I was growing up, I struggled with a stuttering issue whenever I felt nervous or excited. It's a quirk my husband still finds endearing, and he smiles whenever it resurfaces. During my early years on the show, I noticed I would start stumbling over my words during media interviews. I could see the disappointment on my face as if I had let myself down. Watching or listening to myself became unbearable when the promoters or publicists sent us links to our interviews.

Although speech therapy may have been a possibility during my younger years, now that I found myself in the spotlight, I had no choice but to set aside any self-pity and focus on the challenges ahead. So, I developed a technique to help me cope. Before each interview, I would take deep breaths and focus on channeling my excitement into my facial expressions rather than rushing through my dialogue. In my seven years, I noticed a tremendous improvement to the point where I no longer stuttered when doing media. Nevertheless, I thoroughly examined every interview to identify areas for improvement and strive for even greater success.

Our professional and personal responsibility was to devote every ounce of energy to every performance, public relations appearance, and interaction with the audience. During the two-year tour, we never failed to astound audiences with our awe-inspiring show, performing it an incredible 1,000 times. While it may have been our 734th show, for the audience, it could have been their very first and possibly only opportunity to experience the enchantment of The Greatest Show On Earth. As someone living out their childhood dream, I couldn't fathom giving anything less to my audience. This realization shifted my perspective - my performance was never solely about me; it was about the audience. Each night, I felt a deep sense of responsibility to entertain the 17,000 individuals in the crowd.

My position was so coveted that many people only dreamed about it. In many of the cities we visited, I'd run into those who had the ambition to be on Ringling and truly desired it. They looked up to me and the other clowns and saw us as "Clown Gods" in their eyes; I, too, had similar feelings once and related to their wants and desires. I stood in the place of those before me and knew I had to exceed these high expectations.

We often hear of people who, upon meeting their childhood idols, experience disillusionment once the encounter concludes. I never wanted to be that statistic and always made time to chat with those who idolized us in our coveted careers. Earlier, I mentioned the obligation we have in life to pursue what inspires us, to **DREAM big**. For me, that meant leaving no room for mediocrity. Given such a remarkable opportunity, or "golden key," it was imperative to continuously improve my skills and make the most of this time.

Towards the end of my rookie year with the show, I experienced my first contract negotiations with Tim Holst. Dancers and clowns were on a year-by-year contract, and acts would either sign a two or multi-show contract. Before the contract negotiations in 2006, show management had fired two female clowns from Hungary for their conduct on and off the floor. They had graduated from the prestigious Budapest Circus School before joining Ringling and were initially hired as jugglers. They were undeniably talented and performed an impressive juggling and hand-balancing routine. However, never having clowned before, they lacked the specific skills expected of professional clowns, and their backstage antics overshadowed their performance on the arena floor.

TIM HOLST AND I DURING REHEARSALS, 2007

November 19, 2006

Dear Dustin,

I would like to thank you for all of your hard work this past season. It is because of performers like you that we continue to be the "Greatest Show on Earth".

Congratulations!

Tim Holst

DURING THE FINAL PERFORMANCE OF MY FIRST YEAR, TIM HOLST HAND-DELIVERED A LETTER TO ME. I WAS THE ONLY ONE WHO HAD EVER RECEIVED A LETTER LIKE THIS FROM TIM.

Although I acknowledged their flaws, I refrained from explicitly expressing my opinion about them or any other artists to anyone, as it was not my prerogative. When the time came for me to sit down with Tim to discuss my first year and the potential offer of a second-year contract, he posed a question that still resonates with me. He asked me, "What do you think of the clowns from Hungary?" Without hesitation, I responded, "I don't know. I'm too focused on myself to worry about them or anyone else." To my surprise, Tim replied, "Good answer."

I can't help but cringe at what could have transpired if I had divulged my thoughts. It was a valuable lesson in minding your own business and prioritizing self-focus. Focusing on ourselves allows things to fall into place naturally, eventually exposing those who lack genuine passion for their roles.

It's quite easy to get entangled in the politics of your work environment; I speak from a personal experience. There should have been a chapter in this book titled, "Balancing on the Highwire of Corporate Politics." If there's one thing I learned and still hold on to, it is to realize that immersing oneself in the toxic environment of workplace politics only harms you and your character. While resisting the urge to worry about why someone else isn't pulling their weight may be challenging, rest assured that it is in your best interest to focus on what you can change and achieve. Let my experience of prioritizing self-improvement serve as a lesson to pick your battles carefully.

The following year in September 2007, during contract negotiations, Tim approached me and offered the opportunity to step into the role of the Boss Clown, or manager of the clowns. I was in utter disbelief and overwhelmed with excitement at this opportunity. As much as I wanted to take the helm of the clowns, I had a strong intuition that it wasn't the right time for me to take on such a significant responsibility. I remember telling Tim I wasn't quite ready but assured him I would be prepared for the role by the following year.

During the subsequent year, I took full ownership of my role in the show and embraced a more senior clown position. I arrived at the arena early, diligently practiced my skills, and eagerly participated in numerous publicity appointments. My primary goal was to prove to myself that I had the ability to excel as the Boss Clown and fully embody the role.

Later that year, at 22, I was the third youngest individual to be promoted to the position of Boss Clown in the 147-year history of the show. Becoming the Boss Clown had always been one of my aspirations. The position was both physically and mentally challenging as it involved overseeing various aspects of production management.

The Responsibilities of Boss Clown Included:

- Supervising the creation of new and original routines for upcoming shows.

- Managing day-to-day operations while on tour.

- Coordinating public relations appearances.

- Leading brush-up rehearsals.

- Nurturing the growth of rookie clowns (referred to as "First of Mays").

- Maintaining the integrity of our performances throughout the two-year tour (1,000 shows in all).

PICTURED SIDE BY SIDE ARE PHOTOS FROM A GAG REHEARSAL AND DURING A SHOW.

In this new role, I transitioned from focusing on my creative expression as a performer to managing and nurturing the development of 13 other individuals within the show. You might not know this, but it's a difficult job working with a bunch of clowns whose job is to be an IDIOT! I was deeply committed to my role, and any deviations from the plan - be it someone's firing, a gag going awry during the production, or disagreements amongst fellow clowns - affected me profoundly, more so than the individuals directly involved.

However, during my four-year tenure as the Boss Clown, I quickly realized that I could only exert control over the things within my sphere of influence. This epiphany reminded me of a quote by Brian Tracy, who aptly said, "You cannot control what happens to you, but you can control your attitude toward what happens to you, and in that, you will be mastering change rather than allowing it to master you."

Over the course of time, the significance of the clowns had greatly diminished. In the early days of The Greatest Show on Earth, Clown Alley boasted an astonishing 100 clowns who played prominent roles and were frequently highlighted throughout the performances. However, in the early 90s, Ringling shifted its focus to "headliner" clowns, centering shows around these performers and naming productions after them. As a result, Clown Alley took a backseat, with only a few spots allocated for them during the show.

While on tour, former Ringling clowns frequently visited us, embracing the changes the show had undergone over several decades and glowed with excitement and pride. However, a few would visit and nostalgically lament how things were different in their day. They proudly boasted about having 17 costume changes, numerous clown spots in the show, and the fact that each clown had graduated from Ringling's Clown College, which sadly closed its doors in 1997 after 30 years of operation. Whenever I heard these complaints, it would bring brief feelings of defeat and disappointment. But then, I would quickly regain my faith and contentment in the work we had produced.

As the Boss Clown, I embraced a mission to restore our significance and ensure that the new clowns joining our show understood our profound role in the circus world. They needed to grasp the importance of Ringling and its rich history within the circus community. To achieve this, I prioritized each clown to be well-versed in the legacy of the iconic clowns who had graced the rings before them. By imparting this knowledge, the clowns could genuinely appreciate their place within the show and recognize their powerful impact on the audience.

Within Clown Alley, a hierarchical structure existed. Clowns who had dedicated three or more years to the show were considered "senior clowns." These individuals possessed invaluable experience, knowledge, and wisdom, making them a valuable asset to the new clowns joining the show. It was customary for the rookie clowns or "First of May" to seek guidance and mentorship from the experienced senior clowns.

I had always heard stories about the challenges new clowns faced in gaining acceptance from the seasoned Ringling clowns during the days of the circus under the big top. With a constant influx of new faces, it often took time for the established clowns to warm up to the newcomers, sometimes even going a year without speaking or learning their names, as sort of a "rite of passage." However, once a new clown proved themselves by carrying the torch, the senior clowns would embrace their existence in the alley. Through their unwavering dedication and hard work, the rookies gradually earned the respect and recognition they rightfully deserved.

CLOWN ALLEY DRESSING ROOM LINED WITH EACH CLOWN'S STREAMER TRUNK DURING LOAD-IN.

The traditional "rite of passage" concept never resonated with me. From the beginning, I firmly believed I was responsible for treating every new clown with the utmost respect they deserved, as I would have wanted to be treated. I took it upon myself to create an environment in the alley where everyone felt welcomed and embraced. My mission was to foster positive morale and cultivate a supportive culture within our group.

I firmly believed that allowing drama and unrest backstage was simply unacceptable. While some may thrive on chaos, I always preferred to create a harmonious and zen-like atmosphere among us. When we collaborated and operated in perfect harmony, we consistently delivered outstanding performances, delighting both the audience and our fellow artists.

I quickly learned that managing people is not a one-size-fits-all approach. Each individual has unique quirks and triggers that, if not handled tactfully, could lead to explosive situations. As a new manager, I experienced some of these blow-ups firsthand. I discovered that each team member required a different approach to get the best out of them. With some, I could be more firm.

In contrast, I had to tread carefully with others to bring about the desired changes in their behavior or performance. And then there were those individuals who seemed impossible to please, no matter my approach. In those cases, I gave it my all and tried my best.

However, there came a point in the professional relationship where it became necessary to acknowledge that it was best for both parties, the individual and the show, to part ways.

While it was never enjoyable, many times it became necessary to prioritize the overall morale of Clown Alley.

Clowning is a serious craft that demands discipline and extensive practice. It's not a decision one makes on a whim, saying, "That sounds fun, I'll give it a try." I have witnessed the consequences of such a mindset, and it's never advantageous.

There was an instance where a crew member auditioned and obtained a spot as a clown. During the rehearsal period for the new show, the rookie clown approached me confidently declared, "You know, I am going to become one of those clowns that people talk about for years to come." In that instant, his arrogance caught my attention, and I couldn't help but believe that he wouldn't last long. I distinctly recall thinking, "You're going to be remembered, but not how you want to be."

Regrettably, my intuition proved to be correct.

Over time, his behavior took a turn for the worse, becoming increasingly outrageous and pompous. His attitude created a chaotic atmosphere for both the clowns and myself. The negative influence he had began to taint the group's dynamics, making it clear that his removal from the show was essential to uplift the morale of the other clowns. From his perspective as a crew member, he saw us clowns as simply having fun and failed to grasp the significance of our role in the show. The clown's contribution was nothing more than a joke to him as he never quite took the serious business of being silly to heart. It was truly disheartening to witness the deterioration of our relationship, especially considering the strong bond Brandon and I had shared with him and his wife before all of this unfolded.

MY PARENTS WOULD VISIT ME A FEW TIMES A YEAR WHEN THE SHOW PLAYED NEARBY CITIES.

Thankfully, throughout my time at Ringling, I had the constant support of Brandon, who eventually became my husband in the summer of 2016. Brandon, too, had dreamt of being a clown for Ringling since he was just four years old, growing up in Dallas, TX. He was dedicated to his craft and a valuable asset to me and the show. He approached his performances with the same seriousness and commitment as I did. I feel incredibly fortunate to have had the opportunity to perform alongside him for six years. Brandon was my rock whenever I felt defeated as Boss Clown. He always found ways to lift me, offering unwavering support and motivation to keep pushing forward. Without him by my side, I would have never made it those four years as Boss Clown.

During our break between the first and second years of the tour in late December 2011, I received an urgent call from the Ringling Bros. talent scout. He informed me that the creative team, including Feld Entertainment CEO Kenneth Feld, had decided to choose me as the replacement of one of the headliner clowns immediately after the holiday break. The previous headliner, Stas, a clown from Russia, had suffered a neck injury from a minor car accident during Winter Quarters, the rehearsal period of the show a year prior. He had spent the first year of the tour on and off performing, and the rigorous tour schedule proved too much for his injury.

Becoming a headliner for Ringling Bros. was a dream come true and a significant achievement on my bucket list. I was asked to think about it and decide by the end of the day. It took me less than a second to say yes to this incredible opportunity. This experience pushed me beyond my limits and significantly boosted my confidence.

During the initial few weeks of the tour's second year, I dedicated my time to rehearsing with Vas, the other half of the comedic duo I'd be performing with. We had already established a strong bond after performing together in 500 shows. As our comedic routines were scattered throughout the two-hour show, several segments required my full attention and mastery. In the past, I had covered a few of Stas' spots in 2011 when he first got injured. However, this time, it was up to me to tackle the remaining spots, some of which posed a technical challenge.

With a sense of pride, I took on the headliner role. By July of that year, I was one of three jugglers in a featured juggling act. This opportunity arose due to an injury one of the performers sustained in the act. He had torn his bicep muscle while lifting weights before a show. I know what you might be thinking - so many injuries! It is not uncommon for circus performers to face such setbacks, especially during the intensity of a live performance. Accidents did happen with the high-risk nature of our shows, and unfortunately, they sometimes had devastating consequences.

HERE I AM ALONE IN THE CENTER RING DURING A PERFORMANCE. JUST ME AND 17,000 SCREAMING AUDIENCE MEMBERS!

I've had my fair share of injuries in seven year but quickly learned that no matter how I felt, I had to show up and give it my all. We didn't have understudies, so if we missed a show, it would leave a noticeable void in the performance. In the entertainment world, it's common to understand that "the show must go on" despite extenuating circumstances.

That phrase, "the show must go on," first coined in the circus in the 19th century, is often used in the entertainment industry to emphasize the importance of continuing with a performance, regardless of any challenges or obstacles that may arise. It signifies the commitment and dedication of performers to deliver a memorable experience to their audience, even in the face of adversity. This mindset encourages resilience, adaptability, and teamwork, as everyone involved must work together to ensure the show's success.

In 2012, Brandon and I began to get the itch to leave the show and venture into the world beyond The Greatest Show On Earth. From 19 to 27, I had been confined to the circus rings and experienced all I dreamed of in a short time. We had experienced former Ringling clowns who had expressed a sense of being stuck in their artistic pursuits, finding it hard to break free and start anew once they left the show. Even years or decades later, many still struggled to move on or reinvent their lives outside the circus entirely.

Upon observing the conflicting emotions experienced by those around us, we made a personal vow to resist falling into the same repetitive routine. Brandon and I were committed to departing from the circus before our performances stagnated. Have you ever witnessed someone merely going through the motions in their work? It is truly disheartening and gut-wrenching to witness. I, too, began to experience similar feelings toward my role. Despite the allure of continuous contracts, the comfort of life on the road, the familiarity of the show, our devoted audience, and the esteemed reputation of the Ringling brand, we recognized the significance of exploring fresh opportunities and embracing personal growth. I remind myself that constantly looking over my shoulders hinders my progress toward moving forward.

Battling this dilemma, I requested to meet with Nicole Feld, who at the time was a co-producer for Feld Entertainment and the daughter of the owner. While working on the show, I developed a strong relationship with Nicole and her family. I desired a sincere conversation with her regarding my involvement in the upcoming production, and whether it would offer the artistic challenge I always pursued. We scheduled a meeting a few weeks later when she would visit the show in Fairfax, VA.

When the time came, Nicole and I had a wonderful conversation. As we talked for about half an hour, I realized it was time to step out of my comfort zone in the three rings. I didn't reveal my thoughts to her then; I kept them to myself until I entered contract negotiations in Houston, Texas, later that year. This experience taught me a valuable lesson about following my instincts and recognizing when to move on from any career or company.

MYSELF, RYAN HENNING (SENIOR ELEPHANT HANDLER), AND THE STAR OF THE SHOW, ASIA THE ELEPHANT.

Often, we find ourselves settling into a comfortable routine and becoming complacent in our current work situations. It's important to continuously challenge ourselves and seek opportunities that push us to grow and strive for more extraordinary things. Embracing the unknown and stepping outside our comfort zones can lead to incredible personal and professional growth. So, let go of any self-imposed limitations and dare to do something that scares you. It's important to prioritize actions and choices that align with our long-term goals and well-being. By consistently making choices that benefit our future selves, we can cultivate positive habits and work towards personal growth and success.

I knew trying to surpass the unforgettable year of 2012 would be impossible, so I took a leap of faith and embarked on a new chapter in my life.

IN 2011, I WAS HONORED TO HELP RING THE NASDAQ CLOSING BELL DURING OUR ENGAGEMENT IN NEW YORK CITY AT MADISON SQUARE GARDEN. HERE IS A PHOTO OF ME ON THE TIMES SQUARE SCREEN.

Chapter 3

The CEO's Casting Call: An Unexpected Opportunity

After leaving the the Big Show, I strongly desired to continue performing but was still determining what direction to take. Having been a performer in the most prestigious circus on the planet, entertaining millions of audiences, and achieving my lifelong dreams, it felt unimaginable to think that anything could rival the incredible experience I had.

In my last year on tour, I often pondered whether I had achieved my childhood dream too soon, as it felt like I had reached the peak of my career at Ringling so early that there were no other challenges left to strive for.

2013 was a rollercoaster of experiences, ranging from moments of great triumph to moments of deep despair. I boldly decided to relocate to California to pursue what I believed would be the next big thing: a breakthrough in Hollywood. Upon leaving the circus, I didn't have much saved, but around $12,000 to sustain Brandon and me. I applied for my first credit card at 27 and was approved with a credit limit of $2,500. I maxed out the card buying a Suzuki Forenza with a modest price tag of $2,500. I secured a commercial agent, enrolled in classes at the renowned Groundlings (an improvisation school boasting several Saturday Night Live) alums, and took workshops from a former star clown of Cirque Du Soleil.

I needed a job to help sustain myself, and a few weeks later, I interviewed at a bustling Chipotle in West Hollywood. It was a surreal experience, considering just a few months prior, I was at the pinnacle of my career in the entertainment industry. I found it hard to fathom that I was now interviewing for a quick service job. This transition was a humbling experience to say the least.

During the interview, the general manager asked about my experience with knives as they needed more employees to help prepare food. Being quick-witted, I spontaneously showed my right hand with my pointer finger bent as if it were missing. With great energy, I confidently responded with a resounding "YES." He burst into laughter, and to my surprise, I landed the job. Months later, as he was relocated to another location out-of-state, he approached me and shared that the missing finger bit was why I got the job. It had brought him immense joy and laughter, and he knew I would add a different dynamic to the team. This encounter served as a gentle nudge from the universe, reminding me of the power of humor as a tool in my life's toolbelt.

The days I spent working at Chipotle could have been mundane, especially having just come from the glitz and glamor of the big top. However, I consciously decided to dig deep inside myself, make the best of the situation, and infuse humor into each moment to make the time pass quickly and have fun. I even had coworkers willingly switch shifts to work alongside me, knowing it wouldn't be the average work day. I found ways to make customers laugh during ordering and became a pro at diffusing any tensions that arose when things didn't go according to plan – like running out of a specific product or during busier times of the day when the line was out the door, and ordering took longer.

In embracing humor as a guiding principle, my mission became to make the work environment enjoyable for myself and those around me. By using humor as a tool in my new endeavor, I was able to transform what could have been an ordinary experience into something truly memorable both for me and those around me.

It didn't take long for me to realize that the Los Angeles scene presented its unique challenges. The industry proved fiercely competitive, and the unpredictable nature of success created obstacles to establishing oneself. An inner voice began to whisper that my heart wasn't fully committed to pursuing a career in Hollywood. We can never truly achieve our desires unless our heart aligns with our true desires. As my husband often says, "If it isn't a hell yes, then it's a hell no."

Listening to the powerful whispers of my emotions, I boldly decided to say goodbye to the "City of Angels."

In January of 2014, I found solace in relocating to Tallahassee, FL, to be with Brandon, pursuing his Master's in Screenwriting at Florida State University. While being in Brandon's presence brought me a sense of contentment, I couldn't ignore questioning my purpose and path. This mindset all too often plagues the minds of many individuals, and I was no exception.

As fate would have it, a few months later, I received a surprising call from a friend who owns a production company, specializing in creating shows for theme parks, amongst many other projects. He asked if I was free to fulfill a six-week contract for a physical comedic role at Busch Gardens in Tampa, Florida. Intrigued by the opportunity and nothing else going on, I took on the six-week contract and moved from Tallahassee to Tampa. Around the same time, I discovered a University of South Florida student looking to rent out his room, which coincided perfectly with my temporary stay.

A few weeks into the gig, I received an unexpected call between shows from Cw Wolfe, Global Field Ronald Supervisor for the Ronald McDonald program. He had received my resume and was interested in having me audition for the role of the world-famous redhead. Before receiving this call, I had previously auditioned twice, once in Dallas and once in Houston, but received rejections on both occasions. However, I had heard through informal channels that the Tampa Bay franchises held the program in high regard. They were willing to invest resources where necessary, providing considerable creative freedom to the actor portraying Ronald. He mentioned the audition was in Tampa and needed to secure a plane ticket for me. With a feeling of self-doubt and two failed attempts prior, I agreed to audition but assured him there was no need purchase an airline ticket, having just moved to Tampa. I hadn't packed much for my short-term gig, only the essentials. To this day I'm not quite sure, but I also brought a blue suitcase containing my clown shoes, wardrobe, makeup, and small props; I saw this as a sign from the universe.

A few weeks later, I auditioned alongside seven other hopefuls who had flown in from around the country. The audition was held at a local inner-city school in front of 40 enthusiastic and energetic kids. As each auditionee showed up, I quickly noticed I was the only one in a complete clown look. The others auditioning were either amateur wrestlers and balloon sculptors, and I was the only one with a background in clowning. While we waited for the audition to begin, we were cramped in the principal's office like sardines, anxiously anticipating our time in the spotlight to impress the panel of corporate and franchise judges. Amidst the anticipation, there was one auditionee who paced, repeatedly muttering to himself, "I f***ing suck, I f****ing suck." His self-doubt began to poison the rest of us, so I firmly asked him to please be quiet as his negative energy was beginning to undermine our confidence.

Shaking off the negative energy, I was the first to audition among the group of eight performers. As I took the stage, I delivered my eight-minute performance, and time seemed to fly by remarkably fast. Following my audition, three others showcased their skills before the judges took a break to prepare for the remaining four auditions. I was called to the panel's table for a ten-minute interview before I had to leave, as I had shows at Busch Gardens later that afternoon.

During a series of questions, one particularly stood out: I was asked about my perception of McDonald's and how it might affect my performance. I found this line of questioning rather peculiar. The franchise owner had a valid reason behind their inquiry. They wanted to ensure that the person representing their brand had a positive outlook and could showcase that in their performances. After all, I had lost 127 pounds and committed to a healthier lifestyle.

In hindsight, I appreciate the thoroughness of the interview process. McDonald's needed to select someone with the talent and a genuine enthusiasm for the brand. They wanted someone who could be the face of the company, devoid of any negative perceptions, and actively promote the brand within the community authentically. The following day, I received an offer for the Ronald McDonald contract in the Tampa Bay region.

A few years later I was told that one of the judges was impressed that I could hold a serious business conversation while wearing full clown attire. He had expected me to do "clown tricks" during the interview.

The contract offer was a five-year deal that would have bound me until 2019. Since my previous experience at Ringling involved signing one-year contracts, the thought of committing to such a long-term obligation made me anxious. Not having encountered a Ronald McDonald appearance before and being unsure of the potential challenges, I realized that being locked into a five-year agreement would make it challenging to break free if necessary. Despite the confusion of the owner-operators regarding my decision to decline the five-year deal, they agreed to the year-to-year contract, which pleased me immensely.

After my gig at Busch Gardens Tampa Bay came to an end, I made the transition to the Ronald McDonald program. I had the opportunity to observe and learn from the outgoing actor who had taken on the role for over 30 years in the area. Interestingly, he had been a former print model, earning a living through sports magazine appearances showcasing watercraft before becoming Ronald.

In the program's early days, it was uncommon to find professional clowns portraying Ronald, as many of the guys were models or actors. In the late 80s and early 90s, former clowns from Ringling began to take on the role after leaving the road. The Global Field Ronald Manager, Aye Jaye, would randomly show up at the shows and scout clowns he knew were leaving. During my time on the road, we often heard that being selected as Ronald McDonald was considered the pinnacle, often referred to as the "Cadillac of Clowning."

MY PUBLICITY PHOTO I USED WHEN SIGNING AUTOGRAPHS AT EVENTS.

This opportunity would allow me to become a business owner with complete contract ownership. Unlike being an employee of an advertising agency, I would have the autonomy to make decisions. While working for an advertising agency has its advantages, such as having appearances scheduled for you, it also means being at their mercy and constantly on call. They dictate your schedule, and you are expected to comply.

I was honored to embody the character with a red smile and oversized shoes for the next three and a half years. As time went on, I grew a deep affection for Ronald and admired the values he represented. During this period, Brandon completed film school and joined me in Tampa to help me modernize the program, which desperately needed updates. Together, we created a Tampa Bay Ronald website where appearances could be booked, and Ronald's schedule of events could be viewed.

We gave the Ronald program vehicle a fresh new look and saw a resurgence in popularity, with our calendar being booked six months in advance. The Tampa Bay Ronald program was the first and only program to have the vehicle graphics of "the" Ronald in the market. We worked to rejuvenate and make Ronald appeal to the younger generation, and our efforts were evident to the public. With Brandon's background, we incorporated his talents into the show, which had previously only featured Ronald.

In late 2015, I signed a five-year deal with the program. At contract talks, I negotiated Invisalign (clear braces) for myself. My teeth were not picture quality, and I knew I needed to show my teeth when smiling. That year in negotiations, I mentioned, "If you want Ronald to have a great smile, I'll need to get Invisalign." I was told to put the cost and line item in my contract, and the co-op would fit the bill.

Being the Chief Happiness Officer for a multi-billion dollar organization was an incredible opportunity that I knew came with immense responsibility. I needed to perform at my best consistently. In today's digital age, where every move is documented and shared on social media, I had to be mindful of my appearance, words, and how I posed in photographs. I understood that even the slightest misstep could damage the reputation of a 62-year-old brand and negatively impact over 200,000 employees. I recognized the importance of my role and the influence of positivity it carried. I also made it a personal commitment never to make an appearance that was anything less than exemplary. I paid close attention to every detail, ensuring that my shoes were polished, my red wig was flawless, my makeup was symmetrical, and my costume was free of any stains or rips.

Along with a laundry list of "expectations," I was also responsible for bringing joy to adults who had cherished childhood memories of encountering Ronald McDonald, whether through television or advertisements. I always strived to surpass everyone's expectations during their interaction with me. I made it a point to personally greet and engage with every attendee at an event. I took my role incredibly seriously and honored the rich history of McDonald's and its people. Even the most minor details mattered, such as mastering Ronald's official signature, which consists of eight distinct swirls in his hair. I had to execute every action with finesse and a deliberate intention to preserve the character's integrity.

Hanging out with a new friend during a McDonald's crew event at Busch Gardens Tampa Bay in 2015.

In a calendar year, I made around 230+ appearances per contract, each falling into several categories. These included Ronald McDonald House Charities, grand openings, school shows, parades, hospitals, and other miscellaneous events. Among all these, the visits to children's hospitals were the most emotionally challenging for me. Every time I stepped into a hospital, I never knew what kind of situation or condition I would encounter - it could be a wide range of ailments.

During one visit, I walked into a patient's room around eight or nine years old. I handed him a toy and engaged in my usual routine of entertaining the audience in the room. Laughter filled the air as the child, and his mother had a great time. Suddenly, I heard what sounded like water pouring, like a pipe bursting. To my surprise, it turned out that the child had laughed so hard that he had accidentally relieved himself. The mother took it in good humor, and so did we. We bid our goodbyes and quickly left the room, trying not to make a big deal out of it. It was a one-of-a-kind experience for me because it was the first and only time I knew of when I made someone laugh so hard that they relieved themselves. This encounter highlighted the power of laughter and its profound impact on someone's emotions - whether it be tears of joy or, in this case, an unexpected accident!

From the moment I landed the Ronald gig, I was determined to exceed everyone's expectations and had fixed my focus on becoming the Ronald in the most prestigious event the character had ever been a part of – the annual Macy's Thanksgiving Day Parade in New York City. That dream became a reality in April of 2017 when I received a call from Cw, asking me to be "the" Ronald in the 93rd Macy's Thanksgiving Day Parade. Of course, I jumped at the opportunity to be in one of the largest parades in the United States. They offered to cover all expenses, so we decided to fly a few days early and soak in the sights of the Big Apple.

STRIKING A POSE WITH THE "McKIDS" IN THE PARADE!

That year, a remarkable 4 million people lined the two-and-a-half-mile parade route while an additional 50 million watched from the comfort of their homes. It's an indescribable sensation to travel down the streets of New York City and be recognized by everyone from five to ninety-five. As I stood in the enormous red shoe car, waving to the parade attendees, it felt surreal to witness families on their apartment balconies, people leaning out of windows, and screaming "Ronald" from every side. It was a unique experience where I had the best of both worlds. I had the celebrity status, yet I could easily transition back to being me by removing my red smile, and nobody would know it was me. It was indeed a blessing to have that kind of anonymity.

WAVING TO THE SPECTATORS IN THE 93RD ANNUAL MACY'S THANKSGIVING DAY PARADE IN NEW YORK CITY. WHAT A RUSH!

A couple of days later, filled with excitement, we returned to Tampa to take part in a Christmas parade in a charming small town in Central Florida. I couldn't help but constantly gaze upwards, almost expecting to see towering skyscrapers lining the parade route. It took a conscious effort to remind myself that I was no longer in New York City, with massive crowds. Instead, there were only a few thousand people in attendance.

Later that year, I received the heartbreaking news that the Ronald McDonald program would cease to exist as of January 1, 2018. Brandon and I had recently built a house, got married, and had discussed our desire to adopt. I had three more years on my contract and didn't know what to do.

In disbelief, I immediately contacted Bob Conigliaro, the Vice President of Community Relations at Caspers Company, who greatly supported the program. Caspers Company, which owned 60 locations in Tampa Bay and significantly influenced the McDonald's system, frequently hired us for parades, grand openings, and company events. I felt compelled to inform Bob about the situation since he had been instrumental in handpicking me for this role when I auditioned. He reassured me not to worry and insisted that everything would work out.

After weeks had gone by without any updates about the program's impending closure, Bob called me out of the blue and requested that I visit Caspers' corporate office for a conversation. I entered and anxiously sat, unsure why I had been summoned.

Bob began by explaining that after I had shared the devastating news with him, he spoke with Rudy Garcia, President of Caspers Company. Rudy talked with Blake Casper, CEO of the organization, and suggested it might be an opportune time to bring me on board. Bob then revealed that Caspers planned to create a new position within the department, Community Relations Manager. Furthermore, Bob explained that I would step into his role once he retired. I couldn't believe it. Was this some elaborate joke? I was in utter disbelief.

After spending approximately an hour with Bob, I visited the Rudy's office for a conversation with him, followed by a meeting with Blake. We sat at his marble table, positioned next to the sole window in his corner executive office. Blake reiterated the news about Caspers creating a role for me and assured me I would eventually fill Bob's position once he retired. Caspers had a reputation internally for preparing a "bench" of potential leaders for executives close to retiring by selecting promising individuals and grooming them for future leadership roles.

During our conversation, Blake shared something that still warms my heart. He mentioned how he always observed my remarkable talent for connecting with people and making them feel valued whenever he saw me at events. He said, "You may not have realized it, but every time I witnessed you in action, you were on an audition. I would think, damn, this guy can do so much more than just apply clown makeup." He advised me never to lose my sense of humor, as he believed it was the attribute he admired most in me.

I was at a loss for words, not knowing how to react. Once again, I found myself in a state of absolute shock, and trying to process all the information was overwhelming emotionally. Blake asked if there was anything else I wanted to discuss, and I mustered the courage to say yes. Despite having four years remaining on my five-year contract and receiving a severance from McDonald's, I felt it wasn't appropriate I was being forced to use that money to cover the cost of debranding the program vehicles, especially since the shutting down of the program was out of my control. Surprisingly, Blake agreed, and our conversation came to an end.

Just moments later, as I was driving away from Caspers' corporate office, my phone rang. I was informed that my severance had been increased by an additional $15K to cover the expenses of debranding the vehicles. In that instant, I realized I had discovered a leader who would prioritize my well-being and consistently make ethical choices. It became clear that I had finally found my ideal environment with perfect leadership.

It was an honor to be chosen to join the Community Relations department of such a prestigious company, known for its outstanding work with employees and the community. During the hiring process, it was repeatedly mentioned to me how uncommon it was for Caspers to hire externally, as they highly valued internal promotions. Hiring internally for leadership roles allowed all employees to advance and succeed within the organization rather than be limited to just a few individuals. I also discovered that positions only opened up in the office if someone retired or passed away, so landing this role felt like hitting the jackpot, and I couldn't be happier.

A few invaluable life lessons that have shaped my perspective after this experience:

- It's crucial to remember that you never know who may be watching you or the impact you may have on someone. Whether it's a casual interaction or a more significant encounter, striving to be at your best is essential because you never know when you might be unknowingly auditioning for something more significant. However, it's equally important to remember that authenticity matters above all else. Regardless of the influence or power someone may hold, it's crucial to remain authentic and not hide behind false identities. In any interactions I've ever had, from the C-suite to an hourly employee, it's always been important to remember that I am always me, first and foremost. People possess the remarkable capability to see beyond any pretense and discern the genuine essence of a person, and this is ultimately the most significant aspect.

- I had been given the opportunity of a lifetime, one that could have a positive impact not only within an organization and its employees but also among a larger external audience. Recall the symbolic golden key I mentioned earlier in Chapter 2? Like golden keys, such moments are bestowed upon each of us in our lives, offering us a chance to surpass our perceived limitations and achieve greatness, but only if we remain receptive and embrace these blessings with open hearts and minds.

- Rather than engaging in activities solely to seek rewards, it is essential to prioritize actions that align with your natural inclinations. While recognition is valuable for fostering a healthy company culture and boosting personal self-esteem, it should not be the driving force behind your actions. Instead, seek internal satisfaction by knowing your contributions positively impact the greater good. **IGNITE** *your inner fire* and find happiness while doing what you love. And if you receive acknowledgment for a job well done, embrace the moment and trust that the universe will always reward your efforts when you give your best.

- Use your voice and advocate for yourself. I remember the valuable advice of Bob Conigliaro, who emphasized the importance of self-advocacy. He often said, "Take a moment to look over your shoulder and straight down. What do you see? Your back. You must speak up for yourself and do what's best for you because nobody else will have your back like you." I received the additional dollars necessary to debrand the program vehicles because I spoke up and voiced my concerns. This experience reminds us how many opportunities we miss because we don't use our voices. It was a valuable lesson that taught me never to be silent.

Chapter 4

Corporate Clowning: Cracking Comedy in the Workplace

"Laughter is the shortest distance between two people."
- Victor Borge.

Clowns play a vital role in creating laughter, which is undoubtedly the most crucial aspect of their job, as it is the ultimate reward. When a clown performs authentically, their antics never fail to elicit smiles, laughter, or thunderous applause. Clown routines are strategically placed throughout the show, carefully injecting funny moments that contrast the seriousness and intensity of death-defying acts, ensuring a well-rounded and enjoyable experience for everyone in attendance.

During my time at Ringling, our primary goal was to generate moments of laughter every 10-15 seconds consistently. Laughter re-engaged the audience and ensured their full attention throughout the performance. Clowns flourish on the energy emanating from the audience, as it provides them with instant gratification for a job well done.

Considering how much time we spend at work, creating an environment that is vibrant and filled with laughter is crucial. In a world that often feels saturated with negativity, injecting humor into the workplace has never been more critical. I've experienced the atmosphere of walking into many offices during meetings, and I was startled by how sad and quiet the atmosphere can be. Yuck! It almost felt like stepping into a funeral home; at least there would be a good reason not to hear laughter, unless a clown had died, but that's another story.

It doesn't have to be this way. Bringing humor and laughter into the workplace can have numerous benefits. Not only does it create a more enjoyable and positive atmosphere, but it also boosts morale, enhances teamwork, and improves overall productivity. Incorporating humor at work can increase employee creativity by as much as 12%. I've noticed that organizations with a remarkable culture often have laughter echoing through their halls, as laughter creates an environment where employees feel comfortable being themselves without taking work too seriously.

According to a Gallup survey, the frequency of our laughter dramatically decreases by age 23. Surprisingly, the average four-year-old laughs up to 300 times a day, while the average 40-year-old laughs only three times a day. Additionally, 80% of CFOs acknowledge that a sense of humor is pivotal in how well employees fit into a company's culture.

Who would have thought CFOs would recognize the importance humor makes in shaping an organization's culture? Laughter can relieve stress, foster creativity, and strengthen bonds between colleagues.

Imagine the difference it would make if we incorporated moments of fun and joy into our workdays. It could be as simple as sharing a funny story during a break or organizing team-building activities to encourage camaraderie. Creating a culture of laughter allows us to transform our workplaces into uplifting spaces that foster personal and professional development. Having a sense of humor has even demonstrated its advantages regarding your salary. Interestingly, individuals who incorporate humor into their work are more likely to receive promotions than those who lack a lighthearted approach. So, if you're one for doom and gloom, turn that frown upside down and lighten up!

Throughout my time at Caspers, I prioritized infusing every aspect of my work with laughter. Yes, I knew when to turn it on and off, yet I understood the importance of fostering a positive company culture and boosting morale among our large workforce. Our department was known for fostering a positive atmosphere, and we were always ready to step in whenever needed. Whether organizing employee incentives or throwing office parties, we aimed to keep the environment free of negativity, which wasn't always easy.

I often found myself reversing course on my way to the office and stopping by one of our restaurants for a few hours. There were multiple reasons behind this decision. Firstly, it allowed me to build closer bonds with the employees. By leading conversations with humor, I established a common thread that connected us all. I never wanted the employees to associate my presence with anything negative. It was always about fostering laughter and creating a positive experience.

Additionally, being present in the restaurants allowed me to assist the staff in any way possible. Staffing shortages were common, and by lending a hand, I got to meet new employees and share laughter along the way. Showing up and being present eased tensions among the staff and helped build relationships and create a sense of unity.

I have always regarded my sense of humor as valuable, and Blake recognized its significance for the company and my personal growth when he hired me. I discovered then how vital it is to ***own your ORIGINALITY*** and not conform to your environment. Utilizing my God-given talent, I found ways to incorporate humor into my conversations, breaking down barriers and strengthening my sense of purpose, undoubtedly leaving a lasting impression on those I met.

It is essential to prioritize moments of laughter to cultivate a happier workforce, ultimately contributing to higher customer satisfaction. If you lead a team, I implore you to give it a try. Trust me, it's perfectly fine to let loose and show your playful side. It demonstrates your human side to your team, which many leaders never reveal at work.

Here are some ways to cultivate a culture of humor in the office:

- Lead by example: As a leader, it is essential to set the tone by incorporating humor into your interactions and showing that laughter is both welcome and encouraged. I always strive to include a good laugh in every interaction, which is fundamental to my identity.

- Incorporate humor into communication: Using humor in emails, presentations, and meetings can help lighten the mood and make information more engaging and memorable. For instance, when creating an automatic reply when I headed out for vacation, I would add humor to convey the message. I might say, "If I don't reply, it's most likely because I'm drifting in the middle of the ocean or lost at sea." This approach often elicited responses such as "Too funny!" or "I love your sense of humor." My automatic replies had character and were me, not the standard dull, stale automatic replies we are used to getting.

- Encourage team-building activities: I remember organizing a clay shooting session as a team-building activity. The amount of laughter we had, particularly at the expense of our less accurate shooters, including myself, was truly priceless. We all knew that being the best wasn't the goal, and that didn't matter at all. Activities like this help foster a sense of unity among team members and create opportunities for laughter and enjoyment.

- Foster a lighthearted atmosphere in meetings: Start meetings positively by sharing a funny anecdote or encouraging team members to share jokes or funny stories. You can also incorporate icebreaker activities that promote laughter and help build colleague connections. In my experience, using facial expressions to elicit chuckles or smirks from my colleagues during their presentations helped lighten the mood. Although some may joke, "I'm never looking at you again while I'm presenting." Moments like this add a touch of humor to the overall atmosphere, especially during stressful moments.

- Support a positive work-life balance: Foster a workplace culture that values employees' well-being and encourages them to find moments of laughter and joy outside of work. One way to achieve this is by promoting flexible working hours, allowing individuals to prioritize their responsibilities and interests. Additionally, consider implementing wellness programs that support physical and mental health and organizing social events to enable colleagues to come together and enjoy each other's company. As a personal touch, I made it a point to regularly give the office staff cards. These cards were not necessarily tied to any specific reason or action but instead served to show my appreciation. Sometimes, I would write a message inside like, "You didn't do anything for me to write this. I just felt compelled to say hi." It always brought a smile and made the person feel special, knowing I had taken the time to recognize and acknowledge them through a handwritten card.

The benefits of laughter in the workplace:

- Promotes stress relief: Incorporating laughter into the workplace can lower stress levels and cultivate a positive mindset. Happier employees enable happier clients or customers each time, every time.

- Fosters creativity: Laughing can stimulate the brain and enhance creative thinking, encouraging team members to generate innovative ideas.

- Strengthens teamwork: Creating an environment where laughter is encouraged builds camaraderie among team members and improves overall communication and collaboration.

- Elevates morale: Laughter has the power to uplift team members' spirits and cultivate a workplace atmosphere that is positive and enjoyable.

- Boosts productivity: Integrating laughter into the work routine has been shown to reduce absenteeism and increase productivity by alleviating stress and creating a more motivated workforce.

Remember that while humor can create a positive and energetic workplace, it's essential to be mindful of individual preferences and boundaries. What one person finds amusing, another may not, so it's crucial to consider and respect diverse perspectives. Avoid using inappropriate or offensive humor, such as dirty jokes or mocking colleagues, as this can create a hostile environment. Instead, focus on fostering a culture of laughter that is inclusive, respectful, and uplifting for everyone. From my experience, I've learned that it's easy to hurt someone's feelings unintentionally, but it takes effort to bring joy and laughter. So, give your best and have fun, because life is too short not to.

Chapter 5

The Clown Nose and the Business Suit: A Tale of Two Worlds

The clown nose holds a special significance and is considered the tiniest mask one can wear. I can attest to its immense power as someone who adorned one for over 3,500 shows. Within the world of the clown, the nose is just as important as the shoes, costume, wig, and makeup; it truly defines their unique identity. Forgetting to place it on your nose only to face a glaring crowd of thousands can be a nerve-wracking experience. Similarly, the nose string breaking during a performance can leave one feeling exposed and vulnerable, as if performing without a costume in front of 20,000 people. It's safe to say that the clown's nose truly makes completes the look.

Likewise, and perhaps something you can personally vouch for, is the significance of dressing appropriately in your profession. Numerous contemporary CEOs have embraced the practice of donning a consistent outfit day after day, thereby establishing an iconic image associated with their persona. Steve Jobs, for instance, consciously opted for a uniform comprising a black turtleneck, blue jeans, and New Balance sneakers to reduce decision fatigue and simplify his daily schedule. By removing the need to make insignificant choices about attire, he could channel his energy and concentration toward more significant endeavors, particularly his responsibilities at Apple. Undoubtedly, clothing can significantly influence our self-perception and sense of value.

When representing Caspers Company at events, I understood that my attire not only reflected my self-worth but also represented over 4,000 employees. As an advocate for the company's "Image of Excellence" mantra, I needed to uphold that standard in my appearance. I recognized that if I didn't align with this expectation, it would create insecurity within me, and others could sense this energy. Through my personal experience, I have learned that wearing appropriate attire can instill a sense of pride, passion, and self-worth in an individual.

If you encounter a clown without their signature red nose, you might instinctively feel that something is off and think, "That isn't a real clown." Likewise, it is important to recognize that we often unintentionally develop stereotypes based on initial impressions, especially when it comes to considering someone's chosen attire. These judgments are often formed within the first 20 seconds of encountering someone. In the business world, these first impressions are pivotal in projecting the "ideal image" of professionalism.

Imagine attending a Broadway show where the actors come on stage wearing their "normal" clothes - dirty shoes, torn jeans, and unkempt hair - despite the expensive tickets you purchased. Without a doubt, you would question the cast's professionalism, express your dissatisfaction to the theater management, and likely leave the theater feeling disappointed, even considering writing a scathing review like a renowned theater critic. Wearing appropriate attire sets the stage for a captivating performance while also maintaining a professional image and meeting high standards.

Have you ever noticed how putting on something nice, like a tuxedo, a beautiful dress, a stylish sports coat, watch or piece of jewelry can instantly make us feel a sense of pride and purpose? It's a feeling that transcends borders and cultures! Proper attire can elevate our mood, boost our confidence, and make us feel deserving of respect. You can often gauge someone's self-esteem by observing the way they dress. Next time you go out, try people-watching, and you'll start to notice it, too.

I always strive to present myself at my best, regardless of the situation. Whether I'm working out at the gym or running errands to grab groceries, I take pride in my appearance. It's a reflection of how much I value and appreciate myself. I must admit that it wasn't always this way. During my teenage years, I struggled with a lack of self-confidence to the point where I despised looking at myself in the mirror or in photos. I dressed based on how I felt on the inside, which often meant neglecting my outward appearance. It's a terrible feeling to have such low self-esteem that catching a glimpse of yourself in a mirror brings tears to your eyes. However, once I accepted and embraced who I truly was and made positive changes to my lifestyle, including losing weight, I discovered a newfound sense of self-worth and purpose. It all begins with our mindset.

Have you ever walked into a business and struggled to identify who works there? It's often because the employees have chosen attire that blends in with everyone else, making it difficult to distinguish their roles. Moreover, imagine having an issue at a business and needing to speak to the manager on duty. Suppose the person who approaches you lacks an authoritative presence and is not dressed in a way that immediately signifies their managerial position. In that case, taking them seriously or trusting that the issue will be resolved can be challenging. It's important to remember that how we dress reflects how we want to be perceived and plays a significant role in shaping others' impressions of us.

I always consciously tried to dress in a way that left a lasting impression while representing Caspers. The company placed great importance on their dress code, and for good reason. Jeans were not typically allowed in the office, except for certain special events, which were rare. I understood that the public's perception of McDonald's and its employees was not always favorable. Trust me, I can personally attest to that mindset. Before joining the Golden Arches, I, too, had a negative perception of McDonald's as a dead-end job with no opportunities for growth or ambition. However, that negative stereotype was far from the truth.

Only after assuming the role of Ronald McDonald did I genuinely encounter the remarkable culture and principles that the brand imparts to its employees, particularly at Caspers Company. I was determined to break the negative stereotypes that the general public often associated with working at McDonald's. I made a point of dressing in suits and ties, ensuring that I looked polished and professional. I also paid close attention to my grooming, shaving every morning and getting haircuts every two weeks.

Additionally, I maintained a healthy lifestyle, being mindful of what I ate. Imagine if I walked into an event looking messy and unhealthy. People would immediately stereotype me based on my appearance, assuming that my physical appearance reflected the entire McDonald's brand.

Perception plays a crucial role in shaping our initial impressions of others, which can significantly influence our overall opinions of them. That's why first impressions and our appearance are so vital. It's important to break stereotypes and challenge negative perceptions by presenting ourselves in a way that reflects our professionalism, ambition, dedication, and most importantly, self-esteem. It's vital to dress for the role you've been cast in.

Let's take a moment to review the similarities between the clown nose and the business suit:

- Both serve as a form of "costume": Just as a clown nose is part of a clown's costume, the attire you wear is a costume. They help to define the role we're playing at that particular moment. Tell your audience know who you are!

- Both can represent professionalism in their respective fields. The clown nose is integral to a clown's appearance, just as a business suit is commonly associated with professionalism and formality in the corporate world.

- Both can help establish a distinct identity or character. They play a crucial role in defining and conveying the specific roles that individuals are portraying, whether it's the amusing clown or the serious businessperson.

- Both attract attention: A clown nose catches attention immediately due to its bright color and unusual place in everyday attire. Similarly, a well-tailored business suit can also draw attention, projecting an image of self-respect.

- Both can change a person's behavior: Just as a clown may feel more playful and silly with their nose on, someone might feel more confident when wearing the proper attire.

Chapter 6

Carousel of Cultures: Spinning Together in Harmony

"Coming together is the beginning. Keeping together is progress. Working together is success" - Henry Ford.

The circus's vibrant, eclectic world is a microcosm of the United Nations, with both entities sharing a common foundation of diversity, cooperation, and global representation. Like the United Nations, the circus serves as a melting pot of varied backgrounds, cultures, and talents, demonstrating the power of unity amidst diversity. Just like the United Nations, the circus is a beautiful representation of the celebration of diversity and the power of unity.

However, successful conflict resolution is crucial to the operation of both the circus and the United Nations. With such a diverse group of performers, disagreements do occur. In the circus, for example, we had a troupe comprising over 200 individuals from various nations, each playing a unique role in creating a memorable show. We all had perspectives and opinions, from cast members to technicians, wardrobe to floor crew, operations to production teams. Yet, there was an unspoken agreement among us. When we stepped into the spotlight to perform "The Greatest Show On Earth," our differences cease to exist. We became a united force driven by a singular purpose: to deliver an unforgettable experience to our audience. At that moment, any discord or conflict became insignificant.

Every show, we set aside our disagreements and focused on resolving any conflicts that arose. We understood that the magic of the circus relied on our ability to work together harmoniously. It was our duty to ensure that the audience could escape from reality and immerse themselves in the enchantment of the show. In doing so, we entertained and demonstrated the power of collaboration and the beauty that arises when diverse talents come together. We became a living example of how conflicts can be overcome, and unity can prevail.

Irrespective of the audience's size or the city in which we performed, there was a unifying element that bound them all together - a deep desire for an escape, a moment to be transported into a realm of enchantment and awe within the three rings. In my first year with the circus, the ringmaster would end each show with a powerful song, and its lyrics held a profound message: "We're here saving the day from the everyday."

Those words resonated with me as they captured the essence of breaking free from the monotony and routine of daily life. It was a call to go beyond the ordinary and seek ways to make each day unique and memorable. It spoke of infusing our lives with enthusiasm, determination, and intention in order to generate instances that deviate from the mundane. This pursuit of "saving the day from the everyday" is about finding ways to make our lives more fulfilling and enjoyable. It's about discovering and pursuing our passions, trying new experiences that ignite our souls, or finding joy in the simplest things. It's about infusing our days with a sense of adventure, purpose, and meaning so that even the most ordinary moments become extraordinary.

I often drew parallels between the circus, the United Nations, and Caspers Company. Just as the United Nations brings together nations from all corners of the globe, McDonald's unites people from diverse backgrounds, cultures, and tastes under one roof. Whether in Tokyo, London, or New York, you can always count on those iconic Golden Arches to symbolize a united community. With its vast network and over 200,000 employees from various ethnicities, languages, personalities, beliefs, ideas, and preferences, McDonald's forms a dynamic mosaic of global cultures. It serves as a meeting place where people unite, transcending their differences and sharing a common experience.

In this sense, McDonald's mirrors the United Nations' pursuit of diplomacy and unity. It functions as a harmonious medley, seamlessly working towards one shared goal. Just as the United Nations strives to create a world where nations coexist peacefully, McDonald's cultivates a space where cheeseburger enthusiasts and chicken nugget devotees can coexist perfectly. McDonald's also aligns with the United Nations' commitment to sustainability and responsible practices. Like the United Nations, McDonald's recognizes the importance of safeguarding our planet for future generations. Through initiatives such as recycling, sourcing sustainable ingredients, and reducing waste, McDonald's demonstrates its dedication to being environmentally conscious.

By drawing these connections, we can see that even in seemingly different realms like a circus, the United Nations, and McDonald's, there are underlying themes of unity, diversity, and sustainability. It serves as a reminder that regardless of our backgrounds or industries, we all have the power to come together, make a positive impact, and create a better world for everyone.

However, the essence of McDonald's extends beyond its food and environmental efforts. It has evolved into a cultural phenomenon that defies borders. McDonald's holds an endearing place in our collective consciousness, from its catchy jingles that instantly bring a smile to our faces to the iconic Happy Meal toys that evoke waves of nostalgia. It represents shared experiences, treasured childhood memories, and a sense of belonging and unity.

In your organization, you have the same opportunity and responsibility to create a diverse, inclusive workforce that unlocks potential. Embrace this opportunity with open arms, for it is through the coming together of individuals with different perspectives, ideas, beliefs, talents, and backgrounds that true greatness can be achieved. Resist the temptation to hire solely based on surface-level similarities, such as appearance, thinking, or behavior. Instead, prioritize recruiting individuals who bring a range of skills and experiences. Consider it as weaving a vibrant tapestry of talent that will enrich and propel your organization's culture forward.

In today's hiring "norms," we are so hung up on a college degree. I get it; some careers need one, and we can all agree it is necessary. I couldn't imagine having dental surgery only to discover that the doctor who performed it was a concert pianist. There is nothing wrong with being a concert pianist, as I enjoy a pleasing piano medley, but his fingers should be on the keys of a piano and out my mouth! A diverse life that is well-experienced far outweighs a piece of paper. Let's change the dialogue and use people's strong suits and backgrounds when filling positions within your organization.

In Clown Alley, I prioritized ensuring new hires possessed unique and complementary skill sets. This approach allowed us to become a well-rounded and distinctive group of clowns, each bringing something unique to the group. When selecting your cast or team members, shift the focus from mere credentials to qualities that genuinely enhance a positive and productive work environment. Look beyond academic qualifications and seek out individuals who exhibit sincere enthusiasm for the opportunity, possess excellent communication skills, demonstrate a genuine passion for personal growth and learning, collaborate effectively within a team, and inspire trust. By prioritizing these qualities, you will construct a team that possesses the necessary skills and fosters a harmonious and collaborative work environment. This environment will be the breeding ground for innovation, creativity, and exceptional performances.

Remember, it is not only about assembling a group of individuals with impressive resumes. It is about creating a space where everyone feels valued, empowered, and motivated to give their best. Your place of work must act as a haven for its people. It's a place for them to be themselves authentically and openly. When you achieve this, your team will consistently deliver exceptional results, benefiting your organization and those it serves.

As you embark on the journey of building your company's United Nations, remember to do so with a strong sense of purpose and a commitment to embracing the unique talents and perspectives of each individual. By doing this, you will witness your organization reaching new heights of success, with an added touch of pizzazz.

Chapter 7

The Art of Juggling Our Soft Skills

Soft skills are essential in our personal lives and are a crucial foundation in our profession. They are present in every aspect of our daily interactions, whether we consciously recognize them or not. These innate abilities enable us to connect with others deeply, navigate through various challenges, and ultimately achieve success. Soft skills, often called people skills, hold immense value across all professions and industries as they are vital in establishing effective communication, building strong relationships, and fostering collaboration with coworkers.

Soft skills come into play in our personal lives when we communicate with our loved ones, handle conflicts, or even manage our emotions. They allow us to empathize, actively listen, and express ourselves in a way that promotes understanding and harmony. In our professional lives, soft skills are equally important, if not more. Our aptitude to handle various challenges in a composed and professional manner, including client interactions, contract negotiations, team leadership, and rejection, is heavily influenced by our soft skills.

Soft skills are remarkable because we often utilize and improve them without consciously recognizing them. They become ingrained in our behavior and shape our interactions with others. These skills are as natural and essential to us as blinking our eyes or breathing. They enable us to adapt to different environments, work effectively in teams, solve problems creatively, and demonstrate leadership qualities.

Performing in large arenas presented us performers with unique challenges, primarily due to the vast distance between the circus floor and the audience. As we looked up at the crowd, it became apparent just how far away they were, almost like a colony of ants. However, before the show began, we had the opportunity to interact with the audience up close on the arena floor during the pre-show. This allowed us to use our voices and eye contact to engage with the spectators, as they were only a few feet away and could fully appreciate our intimate performances.

Once the show started, it was a whole new ballgame. We had to rely on our facial expressions and deliberate body movements to ensure the audience could follow our routines easily. Every movement had to be intentional, as excessive actions, known as "spaghetti," were discouraged. This term was coined by the esteemed clown Lou Jacobs, who spent an incredible 60+ years with The Greatest Show On Earth. We aimed to maintain clarity and effectively communicate with the audience despite our distance by minimizing unnecessary movements.

Having transitioned from performing in large arenas to entertaining audiences in the lobbies of local McDonald's as Ronald McDonald, I quickly realized that the exaggerated movements were no longer necessary. However, what remained crucial was intentional movement and facial expressions, as they played a vital role in conveying the story to my audience, who were now within arm's reach.

In light of their significance, I have compiled essential soft skills that are indispensable for individuals seeking success in their careers and professional endeavors. Through the cultivation and refinement of these soft skills, individuals can enhance their overall professional performance, escalate their prospects for career progression, and foster significant connections within the work environment. By acknowledging the importance of these skills and continuously working on their development, individuals can significantly enhance their careers and professional endeavors.

Communication:

Performers:

1. Nonverbal Communication: Performers excel at using their body language, facial expressions, and gestures to convey emotions, portray characters, and captivate the audience. They must have an acute awareness of how their physical presence communicates messages.

2. Verbal Communication: Performers must deliver lines, sing songs, or engage in dialogue with clarity, pronunciation, and appropriate tone. They must project their voice effectively to ensure their message reaches the entire audience.

3. Emotional Expression: Performers communicate emotions through their performances, conveying joy, sadness, anger, or any other sentiment. They must master the art of expressing these emotions authentically, allowing the audience to connect with the story.

4. Audience Engagement: Performers must establish a connection with the audience, making them feel involved and invested in the performance. They use techniques like addressing the audience directly, encouraging participation to create a sense of engagement, and even eye contact. Maintaining eye contact is crucial in this context as it aids in breaking down the fourth wall between performer and audience, effectively immersing them into their world.

Business Professionals:

1. Verbal Communication: Business leaders must be articulate and persuasive in their verbal communication. They must effectively convey their ideas, strategies, and vision to their teams, stakeholders, and clients. Clear and concise communication ensures everyone understands the goals and expectations.

2. Written Communication: Business leaders often need to communicate through written mediums such as emails, reports, presentations, and proposals. They must have strong writing skills to convey information accurately, concisely, and persuasively.

3. Active Listening: Effective communication is two-way; business leaders must be skilled listeners. Active listening allows them to understand the needs, concerns, and perspectives of their team members, customers, and stakeholders. It helps them build rapport, resolve conflicts, and make informed decisions.

4. Persuasion and Influence: Business leaders must persuade others to gain buy-in for their ideas, initiatives, or changes. They must communicate with conviction, present compelling arguments, and adapt their communication style to connect with different individuals and groups.

Performers and business leaders must continually refine their communication skills to excel. They need to understand the nuances of effective communication, adapt their approach to different situations, and continuously seek feedback to enhance their abilities. Strong communication skills enable performers and business leaders to convey their messages, connect with their audiences, and achieve their objectives.

Adaptability:

Performers:

1. Changing Performances: Performers must adapt their performances to different venues, audiences, or artistic requirements. They may need to adjust their choreography, acting, or musical arrangements to suit the specific demands of a new setting. Adapting their performance style allows them to meet the expectations of diverse audiences and create a memorable experience.

2. Handling Unexpected Situations: Performers must be prepared to handle unexpected situations, such as technical difficulties, costume malfunctions, or improvisation during live performances. Being adaptable enables them to think quickly on their feet, make necessary adjustments, and maintain a seamless performance despite unforeseen challenges.

3. Collaborations: Performers frequently collaborate with other artists, such as musicians, dancers, or actors. Adapting to different creative styles, preferences, and working dynamics is essential for successful collaborations. This requires open-mindedness, flexibility, and merging different artistic visions to create a powerful, cohesive performance.

Business Professionals:

1. Changing Market Conditions: Business professionals must navigate a constantly changing business landscape, including market trends, customer preferences, and technological advancements. Adapting to

these changes allows leaders to make informed decisions, adjust strategies, and stay ahead of competitors. Being adaptable helps them identify new opportunities and successfully pivot when necessary.

2. Managing Teams: Working with teams composed of individuals with different backgrounds, skills, and personalities is challenging. Adapting their leadership style to communicate and motivate diverse team members effectively fosters collaboration, enhances productivity, and encourages innovation. Adaptable leaders can adjust their approach based on the needs and strengths of each team member.

3. Dealing with Uncertainty: Business professionals face uncertainty, such as economic fluctuations, regulatory changes, or unexpected crises. Adapting to uncertain situations requires remaining calm, evaluating options, and making agile decisions. Adaptable leaders can pivot their strategies, reassess priorities, and effectively lead their organizations through challenging times.

Adaptability allows individuals to thrive in dynamic environments. It enables performers to deliver outstanding performances regardless of the circumstances and helps business professionals navigate change, seize opportunities, and lead their organizations effectively. By adaptability, performers and business professionals can embrace new challenges, innovate, and succeed in their respective fields.

Resilience:

Performers:

1. Handling Rejection: Performers face rejection during auditions, casting, or competitions. Developing resilience allows them to bounce back from these setbacks, maintain their self-belief, and continue pursuing their artistic goals. Resilient performers view rejection as a learning opportunity, adapt their approach, and persist in pursuing success.

2. Overcoming Performance Challenges: Performers may encounter various challenges during their careers, such as stage fright, technical difficulties, or criticism from audiences or critics. Resilience helps them recover from these setbacks, learn from their mistakes, and improve their skills. They can stay focused, maintain confidence, and deliver exceptional performances despite obstacles.

3. Coping with High Pressure: Performers often face high-pressure situations, such as live performances, auditions with limited preparation time, or demanding rehearsal schedules. Resilience enables them to manage stress effectively, maintain mental and physical well-being, and perform at their best, even under intense pressure.

Business Professionals:

1. Navigating Setbacks: Business professionals inevitably encounter setbacks, such as failed projects, financial losses, or market downturns. Resilient leaders bounce back from these setbacks, learn from their experiences, and adapt their strategies to overcome challenges. They see setbacks as opportunities for growth and use them as stepping stones toward future success.

2. Leading Through Change: Business professionals must often lead their organizations through significant changes, such as mergers, acquisitions, or restructuring. Resilience allows them to manage the uncertainties and complexities during these transitions effectively. Resilient leaders inspire and motivate their teams, maintain a positive outlook, and navigate change confidently, ensuring their organizations' long-term success.

3. Handling Stressful Situations: Business professionals face high-stress levels, such as tight deadlines, demanding stakeholders, or difficult decisions. Resilience helps them cope with stress by maintaining a balanced perspective, practicing self-care, and seeking support when needed. Resilient leaders remain focused, make sound decisions, and inspire their teams even in challenging circumstances.

Resilience enables performers to persevere through rejection, challenges, and high-pressure situations, while business leaders can effectively navigate setbacks, lead through change, and handle stress. Individuals in both fields can maintain their motivation and adaptability by developing resilience and achieving long-term success.

Creativity:

Performers:

1. Artistic Expression: Creativity is at the heart of performers' ability to express themselves artistically. Whether acting, dancing, singing, or playing an instrument, performers use their creativity to bring unique interpretations and emotions to their craft. They continuously explore new ways to interpret roles, develop choreography, or create music, pushing the boundaries of their art form.

2. Improvisation: Performers often encounter unexpected situations or changes during live performances. Creativity allows them to think on their feet, adapt to the circumstances, and develop innovative solutions in the moment. Through improvisation, performers can turn potential mishaps into moments of brilliance, adding an element of surprise and excitement to their performances.

3. Collaborative Projects: Performers frequently collaborate with other artists, such as directors, choreographers, or fellow musicians. Creativity is crucial in these collaborations, as performers contribute their ideas, insights, and perspectives to shape the artistic vision. By bringing their creative abilities to the table, performers enhance the collaborative process and contribute to developing unique and engaging performances.

Business Professionals:

1. Problem Solving: Creativity is essential for business professionals to solve complex problems and find innovative solutions. It enables them

to think outside the box, challenge conventional thinking, and generate fresh ideas. Creative leaders can identify opportunities, overcome obstacles, and develop strategies that differentiate their organizations from competitors.

2. Innovation: Business professionals must constantly innovate to stay competitive in today's dynamic marketplace. Creativity allows them to envision and implement new products, services, or processes that meet evolving customer needs. By fostering a culture of creativity, leaders can encourage their teams to generate innovative ideas, leading to breakthroughs and driving organizational growth.

3. Effective Communication: Creativity is vital in how business professionals communicate their ideas, vision, and strategies. By utilizing creative techniques, such as storytelling, visual aids, or engaging presentations, leaders can captivate and inspire their teams, stakeholders, and customers. Creative communication helps leaders convey complex concepts compellingly and memorably, fostering understanding and buy-in.

Performers use creativity to express themselves artistically, adapt to unexpected situations, and collaborate effectively. Business professionals leverage creativity to solve problems, drive innovation, and communicate effectively. By nurturing and harnessing their creative abilities, individuals in both realms can bring fresh perspectives, originality, and a competitive edge to their work.

Leadership:

Performers:

1. Leading on Stage: Performers often take on leadership roles within their artistic projects. For example, a lead actor or actress may lead the cast and crew during rehearsals and performances, ensuring everyone is on the same page and working towards a common goal. They must inspire and motivate their fellow performers, fostering a collaborative and cohesive environment.

2. Setting Examples: Performers are constantly observed by their peers and audiences. Leaders are responsible for setting examples of professionalism, discipline, and dedication. By consistently demonstrating these qualities in their work, performers inspire others to follow suit and strive for excellence in their artistic endeavors.

3. Supporting and Mentoring: Experienced performers often take on mentorship roles, guiding and supporting younger or less experienced artists. This requires leadership skills such as providing constructive feedback, guidance, and talent nurturing. By sharing their knowledge and experiences, performers help shape the next generation of artists and contribute to the growth of the performing arts community.

Business Professionals:

1. Vision and Direction: Business professionals are responsible for setting a clear vision and direction for their organizations. They define goals, articulate a compelling vision, and create a roadmap to achieve success. Influential leaders inspire and motivate their teams by providing a sense of purpose and direction, just like performers do with their artistic projects.

2. Decision-Making: Performers and business professionals must make critical decisions under pressure. Leaders must analyze information, consider various perspectives, and make informed choices that align with organizational goals. Similarly, performers often make decisions on stage, adapting to unexpected situations or improvising when necessary. Both require a strong sense of leadership to make effective decisions.

3. Team Building and Collaboration: Leadership is vital for building strong teams and fostering collaboration. Business leaders must identify and recruit talented individuals, create a positive and inclusive work environment, and empower their teams to perform at their best. Similarly, performers often work in ensembles or groups, relying on effective leadership to nurture teamwork, trust, and cohesion.

4. Inspiring and Motivating: Both performers and business professionals need the ability to inspire and motivate others. Leaders in both

domains must tap into their emotional intelligence to understand what drives and encourages their team members. By recognizing individual strengths, providing support and encouragement, and creating a positive and engaging work environment, leaders can inspire their teams to achieve their full potential.

Performers demonstrate leadership on stage, in mentoring roles, and by setting examples. Business professionals lead by setting a vision, making decisions, building teams, and inspiring and motivating others. Both roles require the ability to inspire, guide, and bring out the best in others to achieve collective success.

Discipline & Work Ethic:

Performers:

1. Commitment to Practice: Performers must dedicate countless hours to practicing and honing their craft. This requires discipline to follow a structured routine, set goals, and consistently put in the effort to improve. Whether rehearsing lines, perfecting dance routines, or practicing musical instruments, performers must display a strong work ethic to excel in their chosen art form.

2. Meeting Deadlines: Performers often work within strict timelines, whether preparing for a performance or meeting production schedules. They must manage their time effectively, prioritize tasks, and consistently deliver high-quality work on time. This requires discipline and a strong work ethic to stay focused, meet deadlines, and maintain professional standards.

3. Maintaining Physical and Mental Fitness: Performers rely on their physical and mental abilities to perform excellently. They must maintain a disciplined approach to their physical fitness through regular exercise, proper nutrition, and self-care. Additionally, performers must develop mental resilience, discipline their thoughts, and manage stress to perform at their best.

Business Professionals:

1. Goal-Oriented Approach: Business professionals set ambitious goals and work diligently to achieve them. They must develop a disciplined mindset, break down larger objectives into smaller actionable steps, and consistently work towards their targets. A strong work ethic is essential to stay focused and motivated and prioritize tasks effectively.

2. Leading by Example: Leaders play a critical role in setting the tone for their teams. By demonstrating discipline and a strong work ethic, leaders inspire their employees to do the same. When leaders consistently display a commitment to hard work, professionalism, and dedication, they create a culture that encourages and rewards those qualities within the organization.

3. Continuous Learning and Growth: Performers and business professionals must strive for continuous learning and growth. They must stay updated with industry trends, techniques, and developments, as they require discipline to allocate time for learning, seeking out new knowledge, and actively implementing what they learn to improve their skills and stay ahead of the competition.

Discipline and work ethic are parallel skills for performers and business professionals. Both groups must commit to practice, meet deadlines, maintain physical and mental fitness, and demonstrate resilience. Additionally, they must set and work towards goals, lead by example, adapt to challenges, and prioritize continuous learning. Performing and business professionals can achieve excellence in their respective fields by cultivating discipline and a strong work ethic.

Emotional intelligence:

Performers:

1. Self-awareness: Performers must have a deep understanding of their own emotions, strengths, weaknesses, and motivations. This self-

awareness allows them to tap into their authentic emotions and bring depth and sincerity to their performances. It helps them connect with their characters and deliver genuine portrayals. Additionally, self-awareness enables performers to recognize and manage their emotions effectively, enhancing their ability to handle the pressures and demands of their profession.

2. Empathy: Performers need to empathize with the emotions and experiences of their characters and connect with their audience on an emotional level. By understanding and relating to different perspectives, performers can evoke empathy in others and deliver powerful performances. Empathy also enables performers to collaborate effectively with cast members, directors, and other stakeholders, fostering positive relationships and creating a harmonious working environment.

Business Professionals:

1. Self-awareness: Effective professionals must have a deep understanding of their own emotions, strengths, weaknesses, and values. This self-awareness allows them to recognize how emotions impact decision-making, problem-solving, and interactions with others. Leaders can manage their emotions and respond more accurately and empathetically by being aware of their triggers and biases.

2. Empathy: Business professionals who possess empathy can understand and connect with the emotions, needs, and perspectives of their employees, clients, and stakeholders. This ability to step into others' shoes fosters trust, improves communication, and enhances collaboration. Empathetic leaders create a supportive and inclusive work environment where individuals feel valued and understood.

3. Relationship Management: Business professionals must navigate complex relationships. Business leaders guide conflicts, handle difficult conversations, and build strong relationships based on trust and mutual respect.

4. Emotionally Intelligent Decision-Making: Emotional intelligence allows performers and business leaders to make more informed decisions. By considering their own emotions and the emotions of those involved, they can assess situations more accurately and make decisions that are sensitive, fair, and aligned with the needs and values of all parties.

Emotional intelligence involves self-awareness, empathy, relationship management, and emotionally intelligent decision-making. By cultivating emotional intelligence, performers can deliver more authentic and impactful performances, while business leaders can foster positive relationships, make better decisions, and create a supportive work environment.

Chapter 8

The Show Must Go On: Resilience in the Face of Business Challenges

Picture it, COVID, 2020.

I have always considered myself to be incredibly resilient, having overcome challenges such as depression, being overweight, and coming to terms with my sexuality, among others. As a performer, I learned the importance of having a thick skin and quickly bouncing back from setbacks without taking things personally. In show business, you learn to let things roll off your back and move on; be a duck, they say.

However, in March 2020, when the world came to a grinding halt, I truly understood the significance of being resilient.

I was attending the retirement ceremony of the outgoing superintendent of Hillsborough County Public Schools, the seventh-largest school district in the United States. As the event unfolded, news alerts began to flood my notifications about the emergence of the COVID-19 virus and the immediate cause for concern. The gravity of the situation quickly became apparent, and the world was about to embark on an unprecedented journey filled with uncertainty and challenges. Indeed, those were remarkable and turbulent times as the pandemic swept across the globe, impacting every aspect of our lives.

My role encompassed numerous aspects, including engaging actively with community stakeholders on and off-site. A typical week was filled with various responsibilities, including attending meetings, developing new initiatives, organizing community events, and coordinating donations and sponsorships. I took great pride in my busy schedule, with meetings starting as early as 7:00 am and often lasting until 6 pm. On top of that, I would frequently attend business dinners and late-night galas. Our organization was deeply committed to various sectors of the local economy, including government, law enforcement, education, military, nonprofits, and businesses. I often found myself in the community rather than confined to the office environment. I thrived on this dynamic and fulfilling work, knowing I positively impacted the community and our people.

Suddenly, my calendar, once bursting with speaking engagements and networking events, came crashing down. The impact was profound, and I had to adapt to a new reality quickly. The effect of the global situation hit me when my usual 45-minute to an hour drive to the office was cut down to just 25 minutes. It was a stark reminder of the severity of what was happening worldwide. As I arrived at the office, I realized the significant changes unfolding around me. Half of my coworkers had transitioned to remote work, and the office was devoid of the energy it once had.

Company events, employee initiatives, and new projects were all canceled. Our restaurants ran out of coins due to a national shortage, so we had to start buying bags of every denomination from a local vendor and started counting change. The office next to Bob and I was empty, so we turned it into a triage room where we counted coins for hours each day. I even made a sign for the door that read "Bank of Community Relations."

Instead of visiting the locations, I found myself confined behind a computer screen, reminiscent of the little girl from Poltergeist, longing for one of the ghosts to emerge and provide some form of interaction. The emptiness in the office became a perpetual cause of frustration and letdown. The passion and fulfillment I once derived from my work vanished, leaving me devoid of motivation and ambition, merely going through the motions each day.

One evening, as my husband and I sat down for dinner, I couldn't help but express my sadness and creative stagnation. I shared how the office environment had become depressing, and I felt like I wasn't being true to myself and my abilities. It was then that Brandon said something that instantly shifted my perspective. He told me I had two choices: 1.) See COVID as the worst thing that could happen to me professionally, or 2.) Use it as an opportunity to make the best out of the situation.

His words were like a light switch being flipped on. It made me realize I could decide how to respond to these challenging circumstances. I could either let myself be defeated by the circumstances or use this as an opportunity to find new ways to contribute and make a positive impact. From that moment on, I decided to embrace the latter perspective. It was a chance to explore different avenues, tap into my creativity, and make a difference however I could. Rather than being bored and unsure of what to do, I saw it as an opportunity to think outside the box, take on new challenges, and create something meaningful.

Brandon's words reminded me there is always a choice, even in adversity. I saw this situation as a catalyst for personal and professional growth, a chance to adapt and discover new possibilities. With that mindset, I found the resilience and determination to navigate these uncertain times and make a positive impact along the way. The months that followed were truly remarkable. I remember walking into the office each day with a renewed sense of purpose, eager to brainstorm ideas that would allow us to connect with our communities and make a positive impact. Our team collaborated on various initiatives, finding ways to stay relevant during an overwhelmingly irrelevant time.

We created a custom coupon for a free meal and mailed it to over 10,000 law enforcement officers in the surrounding counties as a gesture of appreciation for their dedication and service. We extended the same gesture to the Tampa General Hospital's frontline workers, recognizing their tireless efforts. Seeing how such a simple act of kindness could make a difference was heartwarming.

I took the initiative to organize food donations to local hospitals and assisted living facilities, ensuring that the dedicated staff members were well-supported. We delivered meals from our restaurants daily to these facilities, bringing joy and hope. Additionally, I called my contacts at Cox Media Group, Heart Media, and Beasley Media Group and arranged on-air interviews with local stations. Through these interviews, we were able to promote our community initiatives, emphasizing our commitment to providing free meals for frontline workers at all 51 Tampa Bay locations.

The results of our efforts were truly extraordinary. In just a few months, we donated over 100,000 meals, significantly impacting our community. Beyond the numbers, our initiatives ignited a sense of hope and unity among the locals. Our actions garnered attention from television coverage and sparked a surge of responses on our social media platforms. Moreover, our efforts inspired other restaurants to join us in making a difference. The positive feedback and support we received from our online community was genuinely heartening.

I understood the importance of recognizing and appreciating the hard work and dedication of our restaurant teams. To ensure that they understood the positive impact our company was making in the community, I prioritized sharing our successes with them. We created a "Thank You" video campaign specifically targeting our restaurants to express our gratitude and show them what their efforts had contributed to. These videos reminded our staff of their invaluable contribution to making the 100,000 meal donations a resounding success.

I firmly believed that our 4,000 plus employees working in the restaurants were not just performing tasks like making sandwiches, taking orders, or handing out food; they were bringing happiness to our customers.

Our restaurants needed to understand their significance in providing a sense of familiarity during an unfamiliar time. They were an extension of our department and the true face of Caspers.

In those two months, we provided much-needed nourishment to those in need and demonstrated the power of coming together as a community. Our actions showed we can make a positive difference even in challenging times. The resilience I saw in the company was quite astonishing and emotionally overwhelming. We saw new leaders emerge daily within the restaurants, and I had never witnessed collective resilience before. Instead of viewing the challenges as insurmountable roadblocks, we saw them as opportunities to grow and learn.

When challenges arise, it is crucial to approach them with a solution-focused mindset. This mindset empowers us to maintain a positive outlook and think innovatively to discover practical solutions. Proactivity and decisive action are fundamental aspects of resilience. At Caspers, our leadership understood there was no one-size-fits-all solution with 60 restaurants, each with unique characteristics. Hence, each location had to devise a game plan to ensure its success.

It is vital to acknowledge the significance of cultivating a resilient mindset. Despite the prevailing discouragement caused by the initial impact on sales and profits within the first month, our collective resilience became a game-changer for the entire company. Those who embraced this mindset were better equipped to overcome difficulties and succeed. In our vocabulary, the word "can't" held no place. Even though our once-revered standard operating system (SOP) had to undergo a complete redesign to adapt to the crisis, our restaurant teams exhibited unwavering dedication. Each day brought forth new challenges and obstacles, but their hard work and determination allowed them to uncover ways to conquer and thrive.

In 2020, I experienced significant personal and professional growth and transformation. In August, I received an incredible promotion to the role of Community Relations Director, accompanied by a substantial increase in salary. This achievement was a testament to the unwavering commitment and hard work I dedicated to my role. What made this year even more extraordinary was witnessing the awakening within Caspers. We experienced an unprecedented profit surge through bold and decisive actions, creating a historic milestone in our 62-year history. Any previous sales records were not merely broken; they were utterly crushed, demonstrating the immense potential and power within each of us.

During our company's Christmas party that year, a poignant moment unfolded as Blake Casper took the stage to recognize every employee's hard work and invaluable contributions. In the past, when Blake's father helmed the company, Joe would don a cummerbund at the annual Christmas gathering. The color of his cummerbund held the key to the significance of the bonuses that would be given out.

However, in 2020, Blake made a heartfelt statement: "If my father were here tonight, his cummerbund would be gold." In a profound display of gratitude, he made an announcement that reverberated through the room - all 4,000+ employees would be awarded a well-deserved bonus, a first in the company's history. This appreciation served as a potent reminder that our collective efforts had made a significant impact and that we were all cherished members of the Caspers family.

To this day, I *give* **THANKS** for the incredible year the company and I had. It taught me the importance of proactively embracing my "zone of genius." This concept is the unique combination of talents and passions each individual brings to their work with the heart of joy and fulfillment. By spending a significant portion of my working day in this zone, I could achieve more, feel empowered, and inspire those around me.

Creating a strong support network is crucial when it comes to resilience. You must surround yourself with trusted colleagues, mentors, or advisors who can offer guidance and support during challenging times. Collaborating with others provides fresh perspectives and new ideas and offers emotional support, which can help you overcome obstacles more effectively.

In addition to professional connections, having a significant other who can inspire and motivate you is also vital. They can play a pivotal role in instilling positive change within you. In Brandon's case, he provided the necessary support and encouragement that contributed to my success and growth.

Chapter 9

Sustaining Happiness: Finding Fulfillment Beyond Salary and Title

Sonja Lyubomirsky, an American professor, perfectly sums it up with her definition of happiness: "Happiness can be defined as an enduring state of mind consisting not only of feelings of joy, contentment, and other positive emotions but also of a sense that one's life is meaningful and valued."

From day one at Caspers, I was genuinely grateful for the opportunity to showcase my talents without relying on the extravagant characters I once portrayed. The culture at Caspers was quite exceptional and had a strong foundation. The Casper family, now in its third generation, had been at the heart of the Tampa Bay community since their first location opened in South Tampa on March 7, 1958. The founder, Fritz Casper, was a clothier in Waukegan, IL, and Ray Kroc, the founder of McDonald's Corporation, was his customer. Whenever Ray would go into the back of the shop to get his suits tailored, his attention would be drawn to the impressive trophy fish on the wall. One day, Ray asked Fritz if he had ever fished in Boca Grande, his favorite spot, and the rest was history. A few months later, after some convincing, Fritz packed up the family car, moved to Tampa, and opened the first location in the state.

Caspers was considered a "Legacy" owner as it was one of the first franchises in the country. Their first location in South Tampa was registered as national store number 086. As of 2024, McDonald's Corporation has an impressive global restaurant count of over 40,000. However, what truly impressed me with Caspers was the tenure of employees. The average years of service at the office stood at an astonishing 20 years, and it wasn't hard to find those in the restaurants with equal if not more, years of service. This longevity is a testament to the positive working environment they fostered. I could have seen myself as one of those "lifers" within the company.

During my five years in Community Relations, I had the privilege of truly taking ownership of my role, thanks in large part to the support and guidance of Bob. While he occasionally reigned me in when necessary, he always believed in my abilities and, with the company's trust, allowed me to achieve remarkable feats both within the organization and externally. I vividly recall Bob saying, "It might not work, but if you fail, you'll learn something from it," when I'd have an idea I thought was worthy of pursuing.

While none of us want to do a lousy job or experience failure, there is always an opportunity to thrive, even when things don't go as planned. Some of the initiatives I and my team members pursued may not have turned out as expected, but we always found ways to thrive and explore alternative avenues to ensure our success. I had the resources and support to make a meaningful impact and thrive in the department. Creativity and thinking outside the box allowed me to excel and thrive in this new chapter, leveraging my previous experiences to bring a unique perspective and drive results.

In medicine, Failure to Thrive (FTT) describes a child's inability to meet the expected height and weight gain compared to other children of similar age and gender. Let's imagine if we applied the concept of Failure to Thrive in the business world. At first glance, this may seem counterintuitive, as failure is typically associated with negative emotions such as shame and embarrassment. However, it's essential to recognize that failure can also be a powerful catalyst for growth and learning.

Many successful executives and entrepreneurs have embraced failure as an integral part of their journey toward success. They understand that failure provides invaluable lessons and opportunities for personal and professional development. By embracing failure, we can discover our weaknesses, evaluate our strategies, and make the essential adjustments to thrive. While embracing failure may seem daunting, it is essential to remember that failure is not the end but a stepping stone toward growth and resilience. Failures provide us with valuable insights into ourselves, our abilities, and the world around us. By learning from our mistakes and embracing the lessons they offer, we can pave the way for future success.

With an annual budget of $2 million, we had the resources that allowed us to try bold initiatives that others couldn't afford to risk. One of my favorite initiatives I spearheaded was the creation of the Joe Casper Memorial Scholarship. Considering our size, belief in education, and available funds, I always wondered why Caspers didn't have an internal scholarship program. When I shared the idea with Kim, the Vice President of People and Culture, she loved it, and we decided to name it after Blake's late father, Joe Casper. Joe strongly advocated for education and had previously co-founded the Teacher of the Year Awards for Hillsborough County Public Schools in the mid-80s.

Despite a previous unsuccessful endeavor to establish an internal scholarship years prior to my arrival, I was confident we could make it work. I gathered resources and devised a game plan, ultimately partnering with a local nonprofit to manage the scholarship platform for us. The scholarship awarded $30,000 to 12 employees, allocating $2,500 to each. My goal was to consistently increase the funding yearly, ultimately reaching $100,000 in scholarships annually. If an organization has the means to enhance the lives of its people, it should take genuine action to do so.

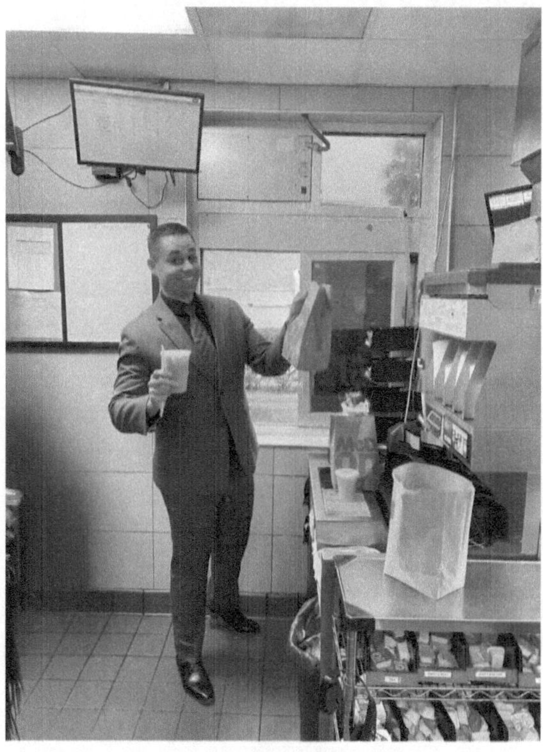

SERVING UP SMILES IN THE DRIVE-THRU BEFORE MY DAY BEGINS!

My role also involved creating and organizing company events and trips, ranging from gatherings of 250 employees to as many as 1,000. We covered various experiences, from manager parties to mini-vacations in Boca Grande and even cruises to Cuba. These events were not just small gestures; we invested significant resources to show our employees that we genuinely cared about them and their contributions to Caspers, with events costing $100,000 to over $230,000 each.

One of my most cherished memories was the annual manager's party in March 2019. We rented out the Florida State Fairgrounds Special Events space. Given my connections to the circus world, it was only fitting to have a circus-themed party titled "The Greatest Managers On Earth!" We had an incredible lineup of talent for the event, including a live circus band playing authentic old-time circus music, the last ringmaster from Ringling Bros., former Ringling clowns, dancers, NBA halftime show acts, a Guinness World Records female juggler, and more. As the event unfolded, Blake approached me and expressed gratitude for a well-done job. He asked, "Did you get an elephant?" I simply replied, "You'll have to wait and see." Moments later, an elephant gracefully entered the circus ring, excitedly causing the crowd to erupt. Blake's jaw dropped as he turned to me with the biggest grin. I knew the team had nailed it.

Understanding and realizing that employees wield significant power now more than ever is crucial. Gone are the days when companies call the shots. With many career paths available, employees can choose where to work and strongly influence company culture and practices. It is crucial for businesses to recognize the shifting power dynamics and understand what employees desire in their ideal workplace.

Employees are actively seeking two vital aspects:

1. Companies investing in their workforce. This simple yet profound action can be done by providing continuous education and training opportunities or offering paths for career advancement. Employees want to work for organizations that prioritize their growth and development, recognizing that investing in employees benefits the

company. Companies can attract and retain top talent by fostering a learning culture and providing avenues for progression.

2. Companies investing in their communities. This is a "rising tide lifting all" approach, where businesses actively contribute to improving the community they operate in. Those seeking employment are conscious of corporate social responsibility and drawn to companies that share their values. By engaging in philanthropy, supporting local initiatives, or implementing sustainable practices, companies can positively impact and attract like-minded individuals passionate about making a difference in their organizations.

We deeply grasped those crucial aspects and worked tirelessly daily to reimagine ourselves and find genuine ways to connect with our people, avoiding anything forced or artificial. Our approach was deliberate and sincere.

OUR TRUE AUTHENTICITY SHINES WHEN WE **INSPIRE, ENTERTAIN, AND LEAD** OTHERS.

Our department had an outstanding reputation for philanthropic efforts both externally and internally, and since the department functioned like a foundation, I rebranded it as Caspers Cares. We emphasized our unwavering commitment to corporate social responsibility, ensuring our customers, community, vendors, suppliers, and, significantly, our employees recognize that we take our responsibilities seriously and handle them with great care.

We acquired a new transit van and enlisted the help of a local vendor to adorn it with the Caspers Cares logo, along with imagery representing the pillars of our giving arm: first responders, nonprofits, and education. This van not only served as a moving billboard as we attended various events throughout Tampa, but it also had a practical purpose. We equipped it with shelving to store our catering equipment and a warming case to keep up to 300 sandwiches fresh and hot. This ensured that the donated food stayed in perfect condition as we transported it from our restaurants to our catered events.

As I embarked on my quest to modernize the brand, I quickly recognized the immense significance of establishing a captivating online presence. In light of this realization, I committed myself to revamping our company website. With an astonishing decade since the website had been updated, it was time to breathe new life into it. Our primary objective was to create an aesthetically pleasing and engaging website that would resonate with our target audience and ensure its utmost relevance in today's fast-paced digital landscape.

During my occasional strolls through the office, enlightening details emerged about outside perception of our department. I would often engage in small talk with other executives. In these casual conversations, some individually expressed their perception of our team as "fractured" or "broken." While I acknowledged that we had some areas that needed improvement, I never bought into the that notion. I firmly believed that each team member had the potential for success and to own their piece of the pie.

While Bob and I had offices with doors, two of our team members had cubicles which left them exposed from all sides, making it easy for others to overhear their conversations and casual one-off comments to one another. However, I knew that with the proper support and encouragement, they could express their concerns and assume responsibility for their positions in the department. It was essential for me to create an environment where each employee felt comfortable openly expressing their disagreements and concerns, as well as empowering each individual to contribute their best.

To create a conducive environment, I held a meeting in a private office, away from the prying eyes of colleagues. I encouraged them to openly communicate their concerns and work towards finding a resolution. It was an intense two-hour session filled with raw emotions. However, they could reconcile their differences through heartfelt conversation and commit to a stronger working partnership. The meeting was a rollercoaster of tears and laughter, but ultimately, it yielded a positive outcome.

This approach fostered a collaborative and empowering environment where everyone felt valued and motivated to strive for success. I witnessed a remarkable transformation within the team as they shifted from simply going through the motions to truly embodying what a team should be. They streamlined their work, making it more efficient and resourceful. I witnessed a shift in their attitudes and a renewed passion for their work. Having a personal connection to your work is crucial in taking ownership of it.

Our team's shift in mindset from pursuing numerous opportunities to prioritizing quality over quantity proved to be a game-changer. We refined our donation requests and reduced the spirit nights we organized with underperforming schools. Streamlining our donation requests made the process more efficient and effective. By focusing our efforts on schools with the greatest potential for success, we maximized the impact of our initiatives. This strategic approach allowed us to allocate our resources more wisely and achieve better outcomes. As a result, we noticed a shift in how our colleagues perceived us. This is a valuable reminder that persistence and patience are essential virtues when striving for long-term success.

Our success was only made possible by a cohesive team of individuals who could set aside their emotions and prioritize the larger goal. Admittedly, there were instances when the way forward seemed uncertain, but we persevered, maintained patience, upheld mutual responsibility, and had fun.

One of my core beliefs was never to become complacent. Unlike many of my colleagues at the office who had worked their way up from a restaurant environment to a coveted position at the corporate office, I entered the company with a fresh perspective and a different background.

One challenge that often arises from being in the same position for an extended period is the tendency to become comfortable in a daily routine. However, my arrival brought a new energy and a fresh set of eyes to the team, which helped to stir the waters and open their eyes to new opportunities. By challenging the status quo and introducing new ideas, we created a culture of growth and exploration within the organization.

Success often demands perseverance and an understanding that the rewards may take time. Having transitioned from the circus, where immediate laughter and applause were the measure of my success, I had to undergo a significant adjustment. It took time to realize that the seeds I planted needed time to grow and bear fruit. During my early days at Caspers, I found myself in Bob's office, sharing my frustration about not receiving immediate validation for my work. Bob, with a smile on his face, turned away from his computer and reminded me of a valuable lesson: we shouldn't rely on others' validation to know that we're doing our best. We needed to trust and believe in ourselves.

Transitioning from an industry that thrived on instant gratification to one that required patience was challenging. However, I quickly realized that the actual value of my efforts lay in the long-term outcomes. Watching the seeds I planted sprout over time and eventually, yield a bountiful harvest brought me immense joy and fulfillment.

This experience is a gentle reminder that success doesn't always happen overnight; it often demands patience and persistence. By embracing the journey and recognizing the personal growth that comes with it, we can appreciate the true worth of our endeavors and find fulfillment in the lasting rewards that success brings. By staying dedicated and keeping our eyes fixed on the ultimate goal, we were able to enjoy significant dividends in the end.

Throughout my tenure at the company, I always placed great importance on my work and understood the profound impact it had. I realized that true fulfillment in life cannot be measured solely by salary or job title. This epiphany struck me deeply when I found myself unemployed during the summer of 2022. It was early July when my phone rang, and to my surprise, it was a Tampa City Councilman with whom I had developed a strong professional rapport. He inquired about a rumor he had heard about the company's intention to sell its restaurants. Initially, I dismissed the news, unable to fully grasp its implications. However, deep down, a nagging feeling suggested it might be true. In response, I promptly approached the Controller of Caspers and relayed the information, quickly reaching the CFO's attention. Within minutes, the CFO stood in my doorway, seeking to understand the situation. Ten minutes later, I found myself seated in Blake's office, completely taken aback by the shocking revelations I had just heard.

The Casper family had decided to sell their 60 McDonald's locations back to the corporation. Out of the over 4,000 employees, I was among the first six individuals to be informed of this significant development. Blake and I had agreed to meet a month later, allowing me some time to gather my thoughts and prepare for what lay ahead. Just a month prior, Bob had announced his retirement, and I had been poised to step into his role on January 1, 2023. With this impending acquisition of the 60 restaurants, I spent the next month engaged in a flurry of meetings with various private family foundations and organizations.

These discussions were crucial in understanding how my role would evolve after the sale. Over three intense weeks, I had more than 20 meetings, meticulously crafting a plan that I believed would be nothing short of brilliant. I even went as far as designing a logo for a family foundation and brainstorming unique ideas for each entity's philanthropic endeavors. Outside the McDonald's brand, the Casper family had other restaurants and concepts for which I generated ideas. A few days before our meeting, I shared my ideas with Blake via email.

Finally, on August 12 at 2 pm, the long-awaited moment arrived. I closed the door behind me and took a seat at the same conference table where I had been welcomed into the organization five years prior. It felt as though this moment had come full circle. As Blake read through the daily sales report and without glancing in my direction, he uttered words that filled me with an overwhelming sense of excitement. "Dustin, I must say, I am incredibly impressed by what you have proposed." The thrill coursed through my veins, and I was convinced that I had secured my future at Caspers. But then, in a single devastating sentence, he shattered my hopes. "You know, over the past month, I've had to say a lot of goodbyes, and I'm afraid this is one of those." My heart sank deep into my chest, and it felt like I could have melted into the leather chair I was seated in.

After briefly explaining my departure, he said it was time to seek a new environment where I could spread my wings and thrive. As one of the individuals entrusted with managing an annual philanthropic budget of $2 million, the company had decided to eliminate my position and department in their quest to redefine their identity and purpose post-McDonald's.

A wave of uncertainty and self-doubt washed over me, leaving me mentally drained. However, I swiftly took action by contacting a professional resume writer from another state and gathering letters of recommendation from esteemed individuals with whom I had forged connections.

A month later, I left Caspers and secured a new job as Vice President with a higher salary; I quickly came to a profound realization. Despite the external allure of financial gain and a prestigious title, I yearned for a deeper sense of fulfillment and purpose in my work, as I had experienced at Caspers. It didn't take long for me to sense a decline in my mental well-being and overall satisfaction in this new role. I felt confined and devoid of the creative freedom I had once had. The culture within the new organization was disheartening and dreary, casting a shadow over my professional experience. It felt as though I had regressed to my formative years, constantly under surveillance and restricted in my actions. When phrases like "I can't wait for the weekend" inadvertently slipped from my lips, I knew a significant problem had arisen.

Within the first few weeks, every employee seemed to seek me out, eager to engage in conversation. They shared their struggles and frustrations, expressing their longing for a change in direction. It became evident that they looked to me for guidance, hoping that I could help steer the organization towards a more positive and fulfilling culture. Through eye-opening interactions with the CEO, it became clear that it was impossible to bring about a cultural transformation and reverse the situation single-handedly. The decision to leave became straightforward and uncomplicated.

One Saturday in early November 2022, a trusted friend unexpectedly reached out to me with an urgent tone. She confided in me, saying something she had never said to anyone before. She expressed concern that my hard-earned reputation and good name would be at risk if I stayed with my current employer. She believed it was essential for me to leave immediately. At that moment, the appeal of a high-paying job and an impressive title as Vice President didn't hold the same importance as my personal well-being, contentment, reputation, and, most importantly, my happiness.

The following week, I decided to resign from my position. We often use the phrase "a weight lifted off your shoulders" to describe the feeling of letting go of unnecessary burdens. I can personally attest to the truth of this saying. Once I handed in my resignation letter to the CEO, I felt an immediate release of pressure and mental stagnation. I had discovered a new sense of purpose and a renewed zest for life.

When I give presentations to high school or college students, I often inquire about their aspirations once they graduate. I ask them if they envision earning a six-figure salary and driving a Mercedes. It's fascinating to witness that nearly all of them enthusiastically raise their hands, except for a few who may perceive the question as ignorant. After all, it's only natural to desire such accomplishments and luxuries. I then explain to them that true satisfaction and happiness cannot be found by solely pursuing those things. Money will always elude them, no matter how hard they pursue it. Money cannot bring us happiness nor enhance our productivity in the workplace. While it's true that we all want and need money to sustain our lifestyles, have fun, and pursue our goals, it's never the ultimate fulfillment we seek.

However, it's crucial to recognize the value and significance of our work, as it brings a sense of pride and happiness to our lives. Throughout my unconventional career, I have realized that one constant factor contributing to my overall satisfaction and success is the authentic joy I find in what I do. During the seven years I dedicated to The Greatest Show on Earth, I was never motivated by the amount of money I earned each week, which only amounted to a few hundred dollars. So when reporters asked about our pay during interviews, I often responded with a playful remark like, "Are you kidding me? I pay them!" The truth is, money was never my primary motivation.

My true source of happiness stemmed from my childhood dreams, a deep-seated aspiration, and a genuine desire to bring joy and laughter into people's lives. I was aware that my work contributed to the greater good of humanity through the laughter I elicited and the sense of purpose I felt. I was determined to fulfill a personal wish, to become someone and do something beyond my existence. Throughout our lives, we encounter individuals who radiate the same genuine love for what they do, regardless of their position within an organization.

Whether it's the maintenance worker who approaches their job with enthusiasm, cleaning the floors of a lobby with a smile and a spring in their step, or the grocery store employee who takes a moment to acknowledge you, offer kind words, and wish you a good day while stocking produce – each person has the potential to impact the lives of hundreds, if not thousands positively. Their authentic excitement and passion can create a ripple effect in their workplace, inspiring others to find joy and purpose in their roles.

Dale Carnegie once emphasized the importance of finding joy in our pursuits: "People rarely succeed unless they have fun in what they are doing." As we grow older, why do we often lose the innate happiness we once had as children? However, it is essential to remember that happiness is a personal choice that can never be taken away unless we allow it. We must not find true happiness from others but from within ourselves.

Since leaving Caspers, Bob has become a cherished friend. His life's purpose revolved around prioritizing "generating happiness," a mantra that permeated our conversations, whether held privately, among co-workers, or with colleagues. He believed in this phrase wholeheartedly, including it as a standard sign-off in his emails. Bob's commitment to his mission was evident throughout his tenure at Caspers, and while his role evolved, his unwavering essence remained constant. We should all take a page from Bob's life in how we perceive life's meaning.

Avoid settling for just a "job." In my perspective, jobs provide temporary solutions without offering long-lasting satisfaction. A job is why you go to work, while a career encompasses the culmination of your life's experiences, including education, training, and work history. High school students may choose to work during their summer vacation to earn some extra money, while college students often seek part-time jobs to help with their tuition and living expenses. Instead, aim to discover a life mission (career) and regard it as a meaningful endeavor that inspires you every morning to take purposeful actions and make a positive impact.

Pursue your mission in what brings you the utmost happiness in life. It's your identity. It's who you are. When you're in your element and are damn good at it, it won't seem like work because your emotional statement is in the outcome, the impact, and the significance it brings to those it's benefitting.

While I've had varying roles throughout my life thus far, one constant in my mission has been humor and giving my audience a sense of significance and worth. Humor and making others feel valued will always be my guiding light regardless of my occupation, title, salary, or mission.

When my time at Caspers came to an unexpected end, and I decided to resign from my position at the other organization, I was at a loss and felt stuck. I didn't know what to do or where to go next, and that's perfectly alright. It's important to question our existence and the path we're on in life. I found myself grappling with these existential questions daily. Reinventing oneself is crucial for maintaining mental health and staying relevant in an ever-changing world.

Just like a reptile sheds its skin to grow and evolve, we, too, must shed our old selves to level up and become the person we aspire to be on this earth. Through this process of self-discovery, we uncover our life's mission, and once we do, everything else falls into place. Our actions, goals, and values align harmoniously, propelling us toward a fulfilling and purpose-driven life. So, embrace the uncertainty and reinvention, and trust that the journey will guide you to your intended destination.

While we do not possess specific knowledge regarding what lies beyond our existence after we leave this earth, I firmly believe that we have a single life, a singular chance, an exclusive opportunity to create a life that brings us happiness. Life must not be driven by constant hardship or daily struggle. Through our mindset and everyday actions, we can uncover the genuine essence of happiness in our lives and positively impact those around us with our mere presence.

Remember, God does not set us up for failure.

Chapter 10

The IDIOT's Epiphany: Discovering the Truth and Finding Liberation

During my initial year at Caspers, I found myself retelling my life's story countless times to those with whom I was building a professional relationship. However, I grew tired of the repetition and felt sorry for Bob, who patiently listened to my story hundreds of times. Despite my weariness, I couldn't help but notice the genuine enthusiasm that emanated from Bob's beaming smile each time I shared my story. It became evident that he took immense pride in my accomplishments, even though I struggled to comprehend why. If a highly accomplished executive like Bob could admire and appreciate my unique story, why couldn't I? While Blake wholeheartedly embraced my previous life, and those around me were enthralled by my unconventional past, I struggled to fully comprehend its significance.

When I embarked on a career change, I initially felt compelled to downplay my previous life as a professional clown, treating it as a deep, dark family secret. I was immensely proud of myself to have accomplished my dream, but I also believed that the corporate world would not view me seriously and might even look down upon me. Internally, I was in a constant push-pull between my past and the desire to discover my true identity and what made me unique.

For the longest time, I sought belonging from others. I yearned for their approval and felt content with myself once I received their validation. It took a toll on both my professional and personal life. I eventually realized the detrimental effects of constantly seeking validation from others. Once I came to terms with my authentic self, I learned to fully embrace life and all its possibilities. This realization became an undeniable truth.

Going to the circus, encountering Ronald, or enjoying a meal at McDonald's evokes cherished childhood memories for many people. While I knew that my career paths were unconventional, I didn't fully grasp how the profound impact they had on people until I began to share my story. Every time I recounted my experiences, I witnessed a glow of excitement and a sparkle in their eyes. My accomplishments became a universal bond that instantly connected me with my newfound audience.

On our journey through life, it is easy to get caught up in our thoughts and emotions, which can cause us to lose sight of our incredible potential. We often place limitations on ourselves, narrowing our path and clouding our vision. As a result, we fail to recognize and embrace our unique qualities and talents, which has always lived within us. Unfortunately, not everyone takes the time or goes deep enough within themselves to discover their true identity and what sets them apart from the rest. It took me a year to find peace in openly discussing my past and embracing my individuality.

As I delved into the depths of my past, a profound revelation engulfed me. I had been unjustly undervaluing my worth and neglecting to recognize the true significance of my journey as an entertainer. It became crystal clear that these experiences had immensely enriched my life, even in my corporate role. I started envisioning my new chapter as a grand stage, a platform to unleash my talents and captivate my audience, just as I had done in the past.

This awakening bestowed upon me a profound comprehension of the five fundamental concepts that have perennially shaped my being and exerted an unwavering influence on my very essence. These principles, deeply ingrained within me, are the pillars of my identity and the driving force behind my aspirations and intentionality.

It is truly incredible to observe how the universe has orchestrated every aspect of my career, guiding me to my current position. My experience as a clown with Ringling Brothers laid the groundwork for my role as Ronald McDonald, and ultimately paved the path for my journey at Caspers Company. Now, as a passionate speaker and "Professional IDIOT," I have gained a deep understanding of what truly brings me joy and fulfillment in my life.

I wholeheartedly embrace the life bestowed upon me by a higher power, with all its highs and lows, and I am grateful for the unique experiences that have shaped me into the person I am today. Throughout life's journey, we undergo constant personal growth and self-discovery.

This process of self-discovery is ongoing and continues until our very last breath.

It is a truly liberating experience to fully embrace your true essence and proudly label ourselves as an IDIOT in the most empowering and extraordinary way imaginable.

Within the following chapters, you will embark on a journey of introspection and discovery, delving into the profound examination and contemplation of the five fundamental principles that I have woven throughout the fabric of this book. These principles, deeply rooted within my being, will forever be an intrinsic and indispensable part of my identity.

Chapter 11

IMAGINE your potential: Unleashing the Power Within

IMAGINE *your potential* as an endless horizon, stretching far beyond the limits of your current reality. It is a vast expanse of possibilities and opportunities waiting to be explored and embraced. Within this expansive realm lies the power to transcend your current circumstances, break through barriers, and unleash your true capabilities.

To unlock your potential, you must be willing to go beyond your comfort zone and embrace the unknown. American psychologist, Carol Dweck, recommends doing something your future self would do at least once daily. This action demands a mindset of continuous growth and a commitment to self-improvement despite fear and intimidation. Embrace challenges as opportunities for growth and view failures as stepping stones toward success. When we fail, there is a lesson learned and a newfound perspective we uncover. In the journey to success, failure is often a stepping stone.

Imagine embarking on a transformative journey of self-discovery and self-mastery, unearthing hidden talents, cultivating new skills, and shattering the limits of what you once believed possible. As you navigate this expedition, you will undoubtedly encounter formidable obstacles, which Randy Pausch, a renowned American educator, and Carnegie Mellon University professor, aptly referred to as "brick walls" in his influential book, "The Last Lecture."

Randy's profound insight still resonate deeply and remains etched in my memory since I first encountered his *ABC Special* interview with Diane Sawyer in 2008. Randy said, "The brick walls are there for a reason. The brick walls are not there to keep us out. The brick walls are there to give us a chance to show how badly we want something. Because the brick walls are there to stop the people who don't want it badly enough. They're there to stop the other people."

Drawing inspiration from Randy's words, whenever I encounter an obstacle or confront a seemingly overwhelming "brick wall," I pause and reflect. I question myself: is this aligned with my deepest desires and aspirations? If it does not resonate with my internal passions, the wall is a natural barrier, protecting me from pursuing a path lacking true purpose. Remember my Los Angeles experience and my realization that my heart wasn't truly invested in breaking into Hollywood? If the goal or aspiration aligns with my authentic desires, the wall becomes a feeble impediment, incapable of halting my progress. I am determined to find a way over, under, or around it unyielding in pursuing what truly matters to me.

By embracing this mindset, I have understood that every obstacle encountered is an opportunity for growth, a chance to prove my commitment to myself. I have learned perseverance and resilience are the keys to unlocking my full potential. With each brick wall faced and overcome, I emerge more vital, determined, and capable.

So, envision the vast potential that resides within you. Embrace the challenges, setbacks, and triumphs that undoubtedly lie ahead. Believe unwaveringly in your capabilities and ability to surmount any obstacle. With a steadfast vision, unwavering determination, and an unquenchable thirst for growth, you will unleash the full extent of your potential and achieve remarkable success in every facet of your life. Through these challenges, your potential is truly tested and refined. In adversity, you discover the depths of your resilience, determination, and perseverance. Each setback becomes a valuable lesson, guiding you toward a more substantial, wiser, and resilient version of yourself.

Your potential is not limited to a single area of your life. It encompasses every aspect, from your relationships to your professional endeavors. It is the ability to excel in your chosen field, to make a meaningful impact, and to leave a lasting legacy. It is the capacity to inspire and influence others, to lead with integrity and empathy, and to create positive change in the world.

I've always believed that when you embrace your potential, you commit to never settling for mediocrity but always striving for excellence. It means seeking new knowledge, acquiring new skills, and embracing new experiences. A mindset of curiosity, openness, and a hunger for knowledge propels you forward on your journey.

"When you're green, you're growing. When you're ripe, you rot."
-Ray Kroc, American businessman

In our relentless pursuit of goals and aspirations, it is crucial to maintain a steadfast awareness of the profound significance that lies within the intricate tapestry of experiences we encounter throughout our journey. One can easily become fixated on the final destination as the ultimate measure of success or fulfillment. However, by consistently reminding ourselves of the intrinsic worth and transformative power embedded within the very process of striving, we open ourselves up to a deeper level of appreciation and understanding.

Each step we take, each obstacle we overcome, and each setback we face holds within it invaluable lessons, personal growth, and unforeseen opportunities for self-discovery. Within these seemingly mundane moments, our character is molded, our resilience is tested, and our perspective is broadened. By embracing these moments' inherent beauty and significance, we enhance our personal growth and cultivate a sense of gratitude and contentment.

By shifting our focus from the end goal to the present moment, we invite a sense of mindfulness and presence into our lives. Rather than constantly living in anticipation of the future, we learn to fully embrace and engage with the present, savoring each experience as it unfolds. This shift in perspective allows us to immerse ourselves in the journey, fostering a deeper connection with ourselves, others, and the world around us.

So, remember that the actual value and meaning reside in the intricate and transformative experiences encountered throughout the journey. By doing so, we redefine our notion of success and fulfillment and cultivate a profound appreciation and fulfillment in every step we take toward our ultimate destination.

Chapter 12

DREAM big: Manifesting Your Grandest Visions

Manifesting your grandest visions is a transformative process that allows you to bring your dreams, desires, and aspirations to life. Manifesting your goals and dreams into reality requires tapping into the power of intention, belief, and action. The first step in this process is clearly understanding your true desires and aspirations, which requires profound reflection. By delving into the depths of your being, you can identify your core values and gain a clear vision of the life you want to create for yourself.

During my childhood, I may not have been aware of my ability to manifest or visualize my dreams. Still, I intuitively understood what brought me joy and fulfillment. This pure and untainted desire was the foundation upon which I could construct my aspirations.

However, it takes more than knowing what you want to make your grandest visions a reality. To manifest these dreams, you must whole-heartedly believe in their possibility, which necessitates cultivating a positive mindset and eliminating any self-doubt or limiting beliefs that may hinder your progress. Adopting a mindset of abundance is crucial, allowing yourself to believe that you truly deserve and can achieve your dreams.

When discussing his invention of the lightbulb, Thomas Edison once stated, "I have not failed. I've just found 10,000 ways that won't work." This quote illustrates the importance of perseverance and the willingness to learn from setbacks. It is fascinating to imagine a world without light bulbs, a reality we would face if Edison had abandoned his dreams after a few unsuccessful attempts. His determination and resilience brought us out of darkness and into the light.

Visualization is a powerful tool in the manifestation process. By vividly imagining yourself living your desired life, achieving your goals, and experiencing the emotions associated with your vision, you align your thoughts and feelings with the desired outcome. This action creates a powerful, energetic resonance that attracts the opportunities, resources, and circumstances necessary to manifest your visions.

In addition to the power of visualization, affirmations and positive self-talk play a crucial role in bringing your grandest visions to life. By repeating positive affirmations affirming your beliefs and desires, you can reprogram your subconscious mind and strengthen your confidence in manifesting your dreams. Affirmations are powerful reminders of your capabilities and help you maintain a positive and focused mindset.

The practice of affirmations and positive self-talk is integral to the manifestation process. You are actively rewiring your subconscious mind to support your journey toward manifestation by consistently repeating positive statements that align with your beliefs and desires. This repetition reinforces your confidence and strengthens your belief in realizing your visions.

Affirmations act as guiding lights, reminding you of your capabilities and potential. They serve as constant reminders that you have the power to create the life you desire. By incorporating affirmations into your daily routine, you can cultivate a mindset aligned with your goals and aspirations.

Manifestation goes beyond hope and wishful thinking, necessitating purposeful and inspired action. It entails actively seeking opportunities, making deliberate choices, and taking steps aligning with your vision. Your consistent and wholehearted engagement in these actions demonstrates your unwavering commitment and determination to turn your dreams into reality. Such actions involve seeking knowledge, honing new skills, expanding your network, and seizing any opportunities that come your way.

In contrast, relying solely on hope can be uncertain and lacking in abundance. Hope is set in a scarcity mindset. Instead, having faith and certainty that the medicine is adequate and that you will achieve your quarterly sales goal embodies a mindset of abundance. By shifting your perspective from hope to faith, you empower yourself with confidence and certainty that propels you toward achieving your desired outcomes.

It is important to note that manifesting your grandest visions may take time. Patience, persistence, and resilience are essential qualities in this process. It is crucial to understand that challenges and setbacks may arise. Still, by staying focused, adapting to changes, and learning from failures, you can overcome obstacles and continue moving forward toward the manifestation of your dreams.

Throughout the majority of my journey in writing this book, I dedicated time to reflect on what truly brought me immense joy and fulfillment. Despite several interviews and no promising outcomes, I turned to my faith for guidance. I reached out to the universe, seeking direction towards a path where I could make the most impact.

Time and time again, I was led towards speaking. I had developed a proficiency in this craft. I understood the importance of stage presence, engaging an audience, and utilizing my unique background to my advantage. After all, it's not every day that you come across someone who once portrayed Ronald McDonald.

I also leaned into surrounding myself with a supportive network. Being in the presence of like-minded individuals who believe in my vision and support my journey is invaluable. Seeking mentorship from those who have already achieved similar goals can provide valuable insights and strategies for success.

I refer to this group of supportive friends as my "Board of Directors." These individuals are my trusted allies with whom I can confide and seek guidance. They genuinely want to see me succeed, just as I want the same for them. I intentionally chose to include them in this small circle of support, as it is crucial to have a diverse network of individuals from various backgrounds who can offer guidance and support and even provide constructive criticism when necessary.

Once you have a clear vision, the next step is to believe in the possibility of its manifestation, which requires cultivating a positive mindset, eliminating self-doubt, and limiting beliefs that may hinder your progress. Adopting an attitude of abundance and possibility creates a fertile ground for your visions to take root and flourish.

Visualization plays a crucial role in manifesting your grandest visions. By vividly imagining yourself living your desired life, achieving your goals, and experiencing the emotions associated with your dream, you align your thoughts and feelings with the desired outcome. This helps to create a powerful, energetic resonance that attracts the opportunities, resources, and circumstances necessary to manifest your visions.

Taking inspired action is a crucial step in manifesting. It involves actively pursuing opportunities, making choices, and taking steps that align with your vision. You demonstrate your commitment and determination to realize your dreams by consistently taking action. This action can include seeking knowledge, developing new skills, networking, and seizing opportunities that come your way.

As you progress on your journey of manifesting your grandest visions, it is important to celebrate milestones and acknowledge your successes. Recognizing and appreciating your achievements reinforces a positive mindset and motivates you to **DREAM** *big* and set new goals. Ultimately, manifesting your grandest visions is about living a life of purpose and fulfillment. It involves aligning your actions, choices, and experiences with your values, passions, and aspirations. You create a significant life aligned with your grand visions by staying true to yourself, pursuing what brings you joy and fulfillment, and positively impacting others.

Chapter 13

IGNITE your inner fire: Unleashing Passion and Purpose

Each individual possesses a unique inner fire, a radiant spark of passion and purpose that delineates the essence of their existence. This inner fire is not from having too much beans, but a powerfully glowing flame that has the potential to illuminate even the darkest corners of our lives, guiding us toward our true calling.

Passion alone is not enough; purpose is the other essential component of the equation. Purpose is the reason you exist, the unique contribution you make to the world. Your purpose is your compass, your guide towards a meaningful and fulfilling life. Discovering your purpose requires introspection, reflection, and a willingness to listen to your inner voice. It is about identifying your true value, what you are naturally good at, what the world needs, and what you can be compensated for. When all these elements align, you find your purpose, your true north star.

Igniting your inner fire and aligning your passion with your purpose can significantly impact your life. It liberates your spirit, unlocking a reservoir of untapped potential within you. It brings a sense of direction, motivation, and fulfillment. It fuels your resilience, empowering you to bounce back from setbacks and keep moving forward.

Imagine being in the Rocky Mountains during winter, and inside a log cabin, you have everything you need to start a fire in the fireplace - a match and logs. But instead of taking inspired action and lighting the fire, you sit there, hoping the match and logs will magically ignite themselves. You desperately long for warmth, but without taking action, you're at risk of succumbing to the freezing temperatures and perishing from hypothermia.

The above analogy can be applied to your passions and inner desires. Just like the logs in the fireplace need a match to be lit and provide warmth, your passions require nurturing and pursuit to unlock the richness and fulfillment life offers. You can unlock your life's potential and wholeness by actively igniting the fire within you and fueling the inner spark that motivates and completes you.

When you **IGNITE** *your inner fire*, its effects can have a profound impact on both yourself and those in your vicinity. I have witnessed the power of tapping into one's inner fire and its remarkable impact on others. At Caspers, we embarked on various projects that aimed to make a positive difference in the lives of thousands of people.

During the 2020 holiday season, we made a generous donation of $25,000 to a local nonprofit. This donation ensured 500 struggling families could enjoy Thanksgiving and Christmas dinners and provide presents for Christmas morning. Our custom coupon incentive program also provided over $749,000 worth of food to local school districts in Tampa Bay yearly. This program not only offered valuable assistance but also played a crucial role in fostering positive behavior, character development, and perfect attendance in schools that required additional support.

I have always believed these actions were necessary and something we truly wanted to do. We were driven by a desire to ignite the fire within us, to strive for improvement, and to witness our community thrive. It all starts with us, taking inspired action and nurturing that burning desire. Without it, the motivation simply fades away. It empowers you to live authentically, passionately, and purposefully. The spark lights up your life, making each day a vibrant testament to the incredible potential of the human spirit. Deep within us resides a dormant fire waiting to be set ablaze. It is the source of our passion and purpose, the driving force behind our endeavors.

Here are some ways to help you ignite your inner fire:

- Self-Reflection and Exploration: Reflect on your interests, values, and talents. Consider the activities that bring you joy, make you daydream, and tap into your natural abilities. Reflect on those moments that made you feel truly alive and fulfilled. For me, the ultimate satisfaction comes from the sound of laughter from my audience. Explore different domains, hobbies, and experiences to uncover new passions and expand your perspective.

- Embrace Curiosity and Openness: Be open-minded and curious about the world around you. Allow yourself to explore new interests and experiences, even if they seem unrelated to your passions. Sometimes, unexpected discoveries can ignite new passions or provide fresh insights into existing ones. Embrace the unknown and be willing to go beyond your comfort zone.

- Leverage Strengths and Talents: Identify your strengths and talents, which often align with your passions. Recognize the unique gifts and skills you possess and consider how you can utilize them to pursue your desires. Emphasizing your strengths can enhance your confidence and motivation, allowing you to fully unleash your potential.

- Connect Passion with Purpose: Once you have identified your passions, aligning them with a sense of purpose is crucial. Reflect on the impact you aspire to make in the world and the values you hold dear. Consider how your passions can contribute to addressing societal needs, making a difference in people's lives, or promoting positive change. This alignment between passion and purpose creates a powerful synergy that fuels your motivation and drives you to take meaningful action.

- Set Clear Goals: To unleash your passion and purpose, set clear and achievable goals. Break down your larger objectives into smaller, actionable steps that you can take daily, weekly, or monthly. This approach helps you maintain focus, measure progress, and stay motivated. Regularly reassess and refine your goals as you gain clarity and evolve.

- Overcome Challenges: Challenges are inevitable on the path to unleashing passion and purpose. Embrace them as opportunities for growth and learning. Stay resilient in the face of setbacks, and view failures as stepping stones towards success. Seek support from mentors, friends, or communities that share your interests to gain guidance, encouragement, and inspiration.

- Embody Passion and Purpose in Daily Life: Seek opportunities to integrate your passions into your work, hobbies, relationships, and personal pursuits. Discover ways to creatively and authentically express your passions. Get involved in activities that resonate with your purpose through volunteering, advocacy, or pursuing a career that aligns with your values.

- Continuous Self-Reflection and Growth: Regularly evaluate your goals, values, and aspirations to ensure they align with your evolving self. Embrace change and be open to exploring new passions or adjusting your sense of purpose as you gain new insights and experiences.

Chapter 14

---

own your ORIGINALITY: Celebrating Your Authenticity

Just like the distinctive patterns of stripes on zebras, your talents and abilities are also one-of-a-kind. They have been carefully chosen for you by the universe. Although you may have some similarities with others, it is through expressing and utilizing your unique qualities that you truly stand out, like a radiant diamond shining amidst a rugged landscape.

As a new clown in The Greatest Show On Earth, I often found myself blending into Clown Alley and even within the show. However, I hadn't fully grasped the art of utilizing my unique qualities to make me stand out amidst a cast of over 100 performers and animals. From the audience's perspective, I may have seemed like a mere blip in the grandest of venues, such as Madison Square Garden.

But here's the beauty of it all: discovering and embracing your originality can be a transformative journey. It's about recognizing your brilliance and learning to shine your way. Just as each zebra has its distinct pattern, so do you possess a unique essence that deserves to be celebrated. Your individuality holds the power to captivate and inspire others, leaving an indelible mark on the world.

During a meeting with a CEO, he abruptly said, "Dustin, I believe your superpowers lie in your intentionality and authenticity." I was surprised that after only a few hours of conversing, he had identified my two vital points. While these qualities may be shared by many, they hold a unique significance for me. Like the mystical unicorn, I have learned to harness these powers and embrace my individuality.

In the business world, a unicorn refers to privately held startup companies with a valuation of $1 billion or more. However, when I use the term unicorn, I am referring not to monetary value but to the extraordinary rarity of each human being, including yourself. Just like the mythical creatures that have fascinated our imaginations in tales since the 1200s, I consider every person a unicorn, a true rarity in their own right.

Just as a unicorn stands out from the ordinary, each of us possesses unique qualities and abilities that set us apart. My intentionality and authenticity are the very essence of what makes me a unicorn. Embrace your individuality and let it shine brightly.

During a lecture I delivered to marketing students at the University of South Florida, I posed a thought-provoking question to the class: "How many of you feel the need to hide your true authentic selves when you come to campus?" The room fell silent as the question hung in the air, capturing the attention of the 50 curious minds before me.

To my surprise, a student raised his hand, someone I would have never expected. He appeared to be a popular student with a network of friends who admired him. But behind his confident demeanor, he felt compelled to conceal his true identity at school, keeping others from genuinely seeing him. It saddened me to think that his friends and other students were unaware of who he authentically was. His honesty opened the floodgates, and other students soon began nodding and raising their hands in agreement.

Recognizing the importance of authenticity and not hiding behind pretenses or masks is crucial. This reflection reminded me of my own experiences as a clown. Despite believing that I never hid behind my clown persona, I realized that even as a performer, I had moments when I felt the need to hide my true self.

At an event I attended during my time at Caspers Company, I had a truly eye-opening experience that left a lasting impression. An annual gathering brought together prominent figures from the state, including dignitaries, local officials, and high-ranking executives. As we gathered for the luncheon, the dignitary table was positioned on a raised platform, facing an audience of over 500 people, myself included.

As the dignitaries settled into their seats and the master of ceremony began his welcome remarks, I started eating my lunch. However, when I looked up at the dignitary table before us, my jaw fell open like one of those Warner Bros. cartoon characters. It was like I was staring at a bunch of plastic dolls. It looked as if each dignitary seemed to have undergone a botched botox procedure, resulting in unnaturally frozen, perpetually smiling faces. I couldn't resist staring at their artificial-like features.

At that moment, I felt compelled to capture my thoughts before they faded. I quickly took out my phone and texted myself, ensuring I would never forget this significant moment. When I returned to my office, I channeled my experience into an article titled "There's No Life In Plastic."

The experience I had witnessed was a powerful reminder to embrace my true self, letting go of any masks that may hide my unique qualities and superpowers. Embracing and fully owning our individuality is crucial, just like a performer possesses the talent to enthrall an audience by embracing their genuine and unique self. They can communicate a captivating narrative through their singing, acting, facial expressions, and movements, as the secret lies in delivering an authentic performance that immerses the audience in their world. I realized I needed to embrace my originality and never hide behind any alter ego or facade again.

In my performances, my ultimate aim was to completely immerse the audience, leaving no room for doubt or disbelief. If I lacked conviction in my abilities on stage, how could I expect the audience to believe in me? The key to delivering a genuine, engaging performance is forging a deep connection with the material. We often underestimate the wise nature of people; they can quickly sense when we are not fully embracing our unique selves, often within the first few moments.

Therefore, we must take that initial step towards wholeheartedly embracing our true selves and allowing the world to witness the incredible individuals we are, showcasing the likeness of our creator. People are drawn to who you are rather than what you can offer them, and therein lies the true enchantment to ***own your* ORIGINALITY**.

Chapter 15

give THANKS:
Cultivating a Heart of Gratitude

Years ago, I came across a powerful phrase that completely shifted my perspective and awakened me to the truth of my present circumstances. It asked a simple yet profound question: "Why would the universe give you more if you are not grateful for what you have now?" This thought struck a chord within me, reminding me of the importance of appreciating and valuing the blessings and opportunities that are already present in my life. It served as a powerful reminder to cultivate gratitude and embrace the abundance that surrounds me.

Do you truly value the life you have been given? Can you find gratitude in the small things that bring immense joy to your existence? It is easy to overlook the little moments which contribute to our success. However, embracing a mindset of appreciation can propel us forward in remarkable ways.

Although I have encountered numerous challenges in my life, I genuinely value each "brick wall" as an opportunity for growth. These experiences have shaped me and helped influence the creation of this book. The process of writing this since the summer of 2023 has been a deeply spiritual journey, for which I am immensely thankful.

I am grateful for the individuals who have guided me throughout my life in various situations. Some have been stayed for the voyage, while others entered fleetingly and departed just as quickly. Each one played a vital role in my growth and development, and I consider myself truly fortunate.

Expressing gratitude and saying thank you is a powerful way to show appreciation to the universe, especially when negative thoughts arise. We are all human beings, and in being so, we often find ourselves grappling with negative thoughts; it is, however, essential to realize these thoughts and swiftly banish them as fast as they enter our minds. It's important to understand that negative thoughts outweigh positive ones, so be mindful when they plague your mind.

Throughout the day, I consciously go through my gratitude list verbally. While some items remain the same, I am occasionally taken aback by new additions that appear unexpectedly. Recognizing and appreciating the things and individuals who appear in our lives, even if they come seemingly out of nowhere, is of utmost importance. This practice has a remarkable way of grounding and reconnecting me with my authentic self. I refer to this daily exercise as my "Attitude of Gratitude."

It can be disheartening to realize that only a tiny percentage of the population will achieve their childhood dreams, a staggering 4%. Still, I am one of the fortunate ones to have accomplished their goals despite facing overwhelming odds. I am immensely grateful for the unwavering support and love from my parents, grandparents, family, friends, mentors, colleagues, coworkers, and, most importantly, my husband. Their presence and encouragement have fueled my determination to persevere through moments of doubt and the temptation to give up.

Let's talk about the power of gratitude, even in the face of being ghosted. While it can be disheartening and elicit various emotions, we must recognize that it serves as a signal from the universe, protecting and guiding us towards better paths that align with our true calling. Regardless of who engages in ghosting, it is never acceptable. When it happens from someone in a position of authority, it raises valid concerns about their treatment of others, the absence of a positive company culture, and their ethical principles.

These experiences should be seen as valuable insights into the character and behavior of such individuals. It's crucial to remember that being "ghosted" is never a reflection of your worth. You should never allow others' failure to acknowledge your value to diminish your belief in yourself. For the longest time, I tied my worth and value to someone's unprofessionalism in not responding to emails, voicemails, or text messages. It undeniably hurts and can be discouraging, but remember, you are so much more than that.

We should also appreciate those moments that reveal the true purpose of our existence and the positive impact we can have, even in the briefest interactions with others. During the summer of 2012, I received a call from a close friend who worked as a talented publicist for Feld Entertainment. She told me about an extraordinary opportunity to meet a courageous four-year-old boy named Dyrk Burcie, who was battling cancer in Dallas, Texas. Dyrk's father, a lieutenant in the Dallas Fire Department, had started a sign campaign to show support for his son, and firehouses nationwide had joined in, displaying signs on social media. My friend asked if we would be willing to participate in the "Dyrk Strong" movement and host Dyrk's family after one of our performances. Without hesitation, I eagerly agreed.

We were provided poster boards and all the necessary materials to create a few signs. These signs would be used to warmly welcome the Burcie family for a special meet and greet on the arena floor after one of our evening's performances. Before meeting Dyrk, we were informed that his time was limited and that this would be his last chance to experience The Greatest Show On Earth. Upon receiving this news, the expression on the other clowns' faces will forever be etched in my mind. Their upbeat, positive spirits came crashing down, and you could see their hesitation in smiling when we knew how the story would end with Dyrk. While reminding everyone that this meet and greet was intended to be joyful and uplifting, deep down, I couldn't help but feel a blend of extreme sadness and frustration, questioning why a young child had to face such a challenging battle that would ultimately take his life.

After the audience had left their seats, the clowns, ringmaster, and production management emerged from behind the curtain, greeted by a beaming family. Clearly, the publicist and promoters had gone above and beyond, showering the kids with programs, light-up swords, hats, and even the show's most expensive souvenir, an oversized elephant plush, priced at a whopping $100. It felt like Christmas, Ringling Bros. and Barnum & Bailey style!

The family joined us on the arena floor, and we clowns sat on the ground to engage with Dyrk. We brought our makeshift signs and snapped photos with the family. Dyrk had his favorite stuffed animal with him, which he played with throughout our time together. He wore a bright smile and acted like any other four-year-old child. However, overwhelming sadness washed over me as the meet and greet ended. I knew that our time with Dyrk was ending forever. Tears welled up in my eyes, and the other clowns followed suit. The streaks of black under our eyes, remnants of our tears, were not flattering for us clowns, so we decided it was time to conclude the meet and greet.

The realization that his young life would be cut short, depriving him of experiencing the complete beauty, joy, and love of the world, haunted me deeply. One month later, I received a call that confirmed the heartbreaking news of his passing on September 24, 2012. At that moment, a profound sense of gratitude washed over me. I had been given the honor of bringing a little happiness into his life during an immensely challenging time. It was a responsibility not granted to many, but I had been entrusted with it. Even now, Dyrk occasionally crosses my mind, reminding me to live fully with a thankful heart.

So *give* **THANKS** to these experiences as opportunities for growth, resilience, and self-discovery. They help us refine our own values and surround ourselves with individuals who appreciate and respect us. Keep shining your light, and never let anyone dim your sparkle.

Chapter 16

The Grand Finale:
See You Down the Road:

Within the realm of the circus, a multitude of superstitions are deeply ingrained. Among these beliefs, there is one that is held unwaveringly: the word "last" should never be spoken when making reference to anything associated with the show, as it carries connotations of permanence. Instead, the preferred term is "final."

So now, we have arrived at the final chapter of this idiotic book! Just like the performers in the ring, our lives are a magnificent spectacle. Every day, we step into our existence with the potential to leave an indelible mark on our audience. Our significance lies not in conforming to societal norms or meeting expectations set by others but in embracing our unique talents, perspectives, and, yes, even our idiocy.

Within the pages of this book, we have delved into the freedom and power that comes from embracing our inner IDIOT. We have discovered that it is perfectly acceptable to stumble and fail, for it is through these experiences that we thrive and grow. In entertainment and business, it is the unexpected moments, the quirkiest ideas, and the courage to take risks that lead to monumental success.

In the business world, we are often bombarded with constant teachings that stress the importance of seriousness, calculation, and unwavering focus on productivity and profit. But what if we dared to be different? What if we brought our unique idiocy into the boardroom, allowing our creativity, spontaneity, and sense of humor to shape our decision-making?

Just as a clown captivates an audience with their humor, we too can bring joy to our colleagues, clients, and customers by infusing our work with lightheartedness and authenticity. Let us break free from the shackles of convention and embrace the power of our inner IDIOT. With this genuine authenticity, we will truly shine and leave a lasting impact on our chosen profession. Embracing one's IDIOT goes beyond personal success; it has the power to shape a more vibrant and inclusive world.

The five fundamental concepts—**IMAGINE** *your potential,* **DREAM** *big,* **IGNITE** *your inner fire, own your* **ORIGINALITY,** and *give* **THANKS**—have transformed my life and continue to serve as my guiding principles. They, too, possess the same energetic power to greatly influence your personal growth, professional development, and overall transformation. It is important to note that I am not a licensed doctor (I'm serious!) and cannot determine whether you are now an IDIOT. This introspective journey is one that must embark upon and define for yourself.

Who would have thought that being a former professional clown would have led me to write a book and be the subject matter expert on being an IDIOT? Life has a peculiar way of revealing our true selves and guiding us towards who we were destined to become when we search hard enough.

As we take our final bow on this grand stage of life, let us carry the invaluable lessons we've learned and the courage to be unapologetically ourselves.

You are not an understudy but the shining star of YOUR show.

Celebrate your uniqueness and generously share your gifts with the world. In doing so, you inspire those around you and create a legacy that will continue to illuminate long after the final curtain falls on your life's work. Your sphere of influence will be so magnetic that it will undoubtedly attract those in your life who want to join you in your journey.

I am deeply grateful for joining me in this grand performance. Your significance in this world is immeasurable, and the world eagerly awaits you to witness the brilliance you will create. Step through the curtain, seize the center stage and let your light illuminate brightly. The time for you to step into the spotlight is now.

In the immortal words from the classic 1954 film, "There's No Business Like Show Business"...

"Yesterday they told you, you would not go far,

That night you open and there you are,

Next day on your dressing room they've hung a star

LET'S GO ON WITH THE SHOW!

May this book serve as a constant reminder that, It's Okay To Be An IDIOT!

See you down the road!
- An IDIOT